Understanding

Romeo and Juliet

New and future titles in the Understanding Great Literature series include:

Understanding

Romeo and Juliet

UNDERSTANDING GREAT LITERATURE

Thomas Thrasher

Lucent Books
P.O. Box 289011
San Diego, CA 92198-9011

822.3309a
Rom
THR

3 1257 01395 0638

Library of Congress Cataloging-in-Publication Data

Thrasher, Thomas
Understanding Romeo and Juliet / by Thomas Thrasher.
p. cm. — (Understanding great literature)
Includes bibliographical references and index.
Summary: Discusses the life of William Shakespeare, the history of
Romeo and Juliet, the plot of Romeo and Juliet, the characters of
Romeo and Juliet, and a literary analysis of the play.
ISBN 1-56006-787-X

Copyright 2001 by Lucent Books, Inc.
P.O. Box 289011, San Diego, California 92198-9011

Printed in the U.S.A.

Contents

FOREWORD

"Except for a living man, there is nothing more wonderful than a book!" wrote the widely respected nineteenth-century teacher and writer Charles Kingsley. A book, he continued, "is a message to us from human souls we never saw. And yet these [books] arouse us, terrify us, teach us, comfort us, open our hearts to us as brothers." There are many different kinds of books, of course; and Kingsley was referring mainly to those containing literature—novels, plays, short stories, poems, and so on. In particular, he had in mind those works of literature that were and remain widely popular with readers of all ages and from many walks of life.

Such popularity might be based on one or several factors. On the one hand, a book might be read and studied by people in generation after generation because it is a literary classic, with characters and themes of universal relevance and appeal. Homer's epic poems, the *Iliad* and the *Odyssey*, Chaucer's *Canterbury Tales*, Shakespeare's *Hamlet* and *Romeo and Juliet*, and Dickens's *A Christmas Carol* fall into this category. Some popular books, on the other hand, are more controversial. Mark Twain's *Huckleberry Finn* and J. D. Salinger's *The Catcher in the Rye*, for instance, have their legions of devoted fans who see them as great literature; while others view them as less than worthy because of their racial depictions, profanity, or other factors.

Still another category of popular literature includes realistic modern fiction, including novels such as Robert Cormier's *I Am the Cheese* and S. E. Hinton's *The Outsiders*. Their keen social insights and sharp character portrayals have consistently reached out to and captured the imaginations of many teenagers and young adults; and for this reason they are often assigned and studied in schools.

These and other similar works have become the "old standards" of the literary scene. They are the ones that people most often read, discuss, and study; and each has, by virtue of its content, critical success, or just plain longevity, earned the right to be the subject of a book examining its content. (Some, of course, like the *Iliad* and *Hamlet*, have been the subjects of numerous books already; but their literary stature is so lofty that there can never be too many books about them!) For millions of readers and students in one generation after another, each of these works becomes, in a sense, an adventure in appreciation, enjoyment, and learning.

The main purpose of Lucent's Understanding Great Literature series is to aid the reader in that ongoing literary adventure. Each volume in the series focuses on a single literary work that a majority of critics and teachers view as a classic and/or that is widely studied and discussed in schools. A typical volume first tells why the work in question is important. Then follow detailed overviews of the author's life, the work's historical background, its plot, its characters, and its themes. Numerous quotes from the work, as well as by critics and other experts, are interspersed throughout and carefully documented with footnotes for those who wish to pursue further research. Also included is a list of ideas for essays and other student projects relating to the work, an appendix of literary criticisms and analyses by noted scholars, and a comprehensive annotated bibliography.

The great nineteenth-century American poet Henry David Thoreau once quipped: "Read the best books first, or you may not have a chance to read them at all." For those who are reading or about to read the "best books" in the literary canon, the comprehensive, thorough, and thoughtful volumes of the Understanding Great Literature series are indispensable guides and sources of enrichment.

A Timeless Tragedy

I t has been said that only time can judge art. That is, good art will continue to be relevant and cherished long after its creator has vanished. This is the case with Michaelangelo's Sistine Chapel, Beethoven's Ninth Symphony, and Leonardo da Vinci's *The Last Supper*. The same case can be made for William Shakespeare's *The Tragedy of Romeo and Juliet*.

Romeo and Juliet was first performed for a London audience in 1596 and has continued to rule the stage for the last four hundred years. *Romeo and Juliet* has taken on a life of its own: It has outlasted its author, its audience, and its time. Less than seventy-five years after Shakespeare's death, the poet John Dryden complained that Shakespeare's words and phrases were "scarce intelligible." However, Dryden's comments have been largely forgotten, while Shakespeare's "unintelligible" words have lasting charm. The story of *Romeo and Juliet*, old when Shakespeare wrote it, has continued to thrill audiences as an opera, a Broadway musical, a puppet show, a cartoon, several feature films, and a drama. It has adapted to every age in which it has found itself.

However, *Romeo and Juliet* has not been without con-troversy. While some critics have hailed the play as a tragic masterpiece, others have lambasted it as a pitiful and senti-mental story. Critics have also debated the meaning of *Romeo and Juliet*. Is it a celebration or a condemnation of young love? Some scholars have even argued about whether the play is actually a tragedy.

Despite the arguments of commentators, audiences love *Romeo and Juliet*. What is it about this play that makes it a con-tinual favorite? It has action, comedy, romance and catastrophe. Its plot can be understood by anybody, and its poetry appeals to scholars and sophisticates alike. Young people identify with the teenage lovers and their struggle to be together in spite of their parents. Older people like *Romeo and Juliet* because it reminds them of the passionate days of youth. In short, William Shakespeare's *The Tragedy of Romeo and Juliet* continues to be a popular play because it taps into a common human experience: the heartrending nature of young love.

CHAPTER ONE

The Life of William Shakespeare

W illiam Shakespeare's father, John, was a man of humble origins. The son of a tenant farmer from the village of Snitterfield, he left home to take up an apprenticeship as a glove maker in the nearby town of Stratford-upon-Avon. Little did John Shakespeare know that this action would forever link his surname with that of Stratford, the town that would forever be known as the birthplace of the greatest writer in the English language.

After John Shakespeare finished his apprenticeship (a term of about seven years), he established his own shop in Stratford making gloves and leather goods for the local gentry. He must have done well because there are records of his purchasing land and houses in the surrounding area. As a matter of fact, John Shakespeare first appears in local records on April 29, 1552. He was fined for keeping a dunghill on a corner of his newly acquired property on Henley Street.

When Stratford-upon-Avon received its charter of incorporation from the Crown in 1553, it allowed the town to elect a common council of burgesses and aldermen to manage local affairs. John Shakespeare, in addition to running a thriving business, also began to take a hand in running the town's affairs. In 1556 he was elected ale-taster, a duty that included making sure that bakers made full-weight loaves of bread and that brewers made untainted beer and ale. Two years later, in 1558, John Shakespeare was named a constable (a type of police officer) and it became his job to preserve the peace of the town. Other promotions quickly followed: In 1559 he was named affeeror (an official who decided how much to charge for fines); from 1561 to 1563 he served as a burgess; in 1565 he was elected an alderman; and in 1568 he was chosen to be the bailiff (a position equivalent to a modern mayor). For John Shakespeare, the transformation must have been striking, for a man who came into town a poor apprentice had risen to become one of its most respected citizens.

John Shakespeare married Mary Arden sometime between 1556 and 1558. For John, the marriage would increase his wealth and add a hint of nobility to his otherwise common status. The Ardens, despite a noble heritage, were ordinary folk composed of prosperous farmers and merchants. Mary was the youngest daughter of Robert Arden, and shortly before marrying John, she had inherited a good portion of her father's estate. By marrying John Shakespeare, Mary would receive a degree of status (John was a successful merchant and rising local leader) and a husband who could manage her considerable holdings and provide for their large family.

The Shakespeares had a total of eight children. Mary gave birth to their first daughter, Joan, in 1558. It is unclear what became of Joan, but it is thought that she died while still a baby. The Shakespeares' next child, Margaret, was born in 1562 and died one year later. William Shakespeare was born in 1564. Two years later, William's younger brother Gilbert was born. In 1569, the Shakespeares had another daughter who they also named Joan. This Joan survived her infancy and lived until 1646. The year 1571 saw the birth of another Shakespeare family member, Anne, who died eight years later.

Shakespeare's birthplace in Stratford-upon-Avon, England.

Richard Shakespeare was born in 1574, and the youngest Shakespeare, Edmund, was born in 1580.

The exact date of William Shakespeare's birth is unknown. It is known that he was baptized on April 26, 1564. Tradition holds that he was born on April 23, a reasonable assumption because it was customary for parents to christen their children three days after the birth. Whatever the exact date of William's birth is, one thing is clear: He survived his infancy (remarkable considering that the bubonic plague visited Stratford the following summer, killing about one-sixth of the entire population).

Shakespeare's Education

In Elizabethan England, academic education was a privilege. Typically, only the children of wealthy parents had the time and the opportunity to attend school. Illiteracy was commonplace. Neither John nor Mary Shakespeare could write, but they were not alone. During Queen Elizabeth's reign (1533–1603), 70 percent of all men and 90 percent of all women could not sign their names.

In Stratford, however, education was free to the sons of its burgesses (the town's representatives to Parliament) and aldermen (similar to councilmen), of whom John was one. Given that privilege, he and Mary made sure that their son William could not only read but write his name as well. Male students began to attend classes at the age of five, going first to a "petty" school taught by an abecedarius, or usher. These ushers taught their pupils the alphabet and the Lord's Prayer using a hornbook, a piece of paper framed in wood and covered for protection by a thin layer of transparent horn. The mark of the cross preceded the alphabet, so it was called the "Christ cross-row." William Shakespeare was no doubt remembering his hornbook when he wrote in *Richard III*, "He hearkens after prophecies and dreams, / And from the cross-row plucks the letter G."[1] At seven years of age, after learning the basics in petty school, the students were ready for grammar school.

Based on comments scattered throughout his plays, Shakespeare may not have enjoyed his school years. In *Romeo and Juliet*, he writes, "Love goes toward love as schoolboys from their books, / But love from love, toward school with heavy looks."[2] Gremio, in *The Taming of the Shrew*, returns from Petruchio's troublesome wedding "As willingly e'er I came from school."[3]

Regardless of how Shakespeare felt about his schooling, it provided him the "small Latin and less Greek"[4] that he would need to succeed in his later profession. In grammar school William Shakespeare studied William Lily's *Short Introduction*

The hornbook was used to teach Elizabethan school children the alphabet.

of Grammar. The first half of the book laid out the basics of English grammar while the second part contained the rules for Latin. For moral instruction the students would read, in Latin, Erasmus's *Cato*, the fables of Aesop, the *Metamorphoses* of Ovid, and Plutarch's *Lives*. The course of study also included Greco-Roman playwrights (which introduced young William to classical comedy and the five-act structure of plays), rhetoric (which he used for dramatic effect), logic, and numeration (simple math).

About 1577, John Shakespeare's fortunes began to decline. In 1578, he mortgaged a house and fifty-six acres (part of his wife's inheritance) to his brother-in-law, Lambert Arden, for cash. John was unable to repay the loan, and this part of his wife's inheritance was forever lost. Later that same year he mortgaged another section of Mary's inheritance, some eighty-six acres, for a set term of years. John's financial troubles continued. Over the next few years, he had several fines levied against him by the courts for debt. It got so bad that the onetime alderman could not appear in church "for feare of process [arrest] for debbte."[5]

The young William Shakespeare was directly affected by his father's misfortunes. When he was thirteen, his father withdrew him from grammar school. Nicholas Rowe, one of Shakespeare's earliest biographers, writes that the narrowness of his father's "circumstances, and the want of [William's] assistance at home . . . forc'd his father to withdraw him from thence."[6] The severance from academia makes some modern scholars doubt whether Shakespeare had enough education to have written the plays credited to him. Although no firm conclusion can be drawn about this, it must be pointed out that he did have a basic education (math, grammar, reading, writing, and Latin). It is also conceivable that Shakespeare continued to educate himself after leaving school, a task made easier because of a burgeoning new business called printing.

Marriage and the "Lost Years"

Some researchers speculate that, after John Shakespeare withdrew his son from Stratford's school, William was placed in a noble family as a servant. These scholars believe that it was at this point that Shakespeare was exposed to higher learning and the aristocratic society that he would write about later in his life. However plausible this scenario may be, considering his father's financial circumstances, it is more likely that William worked in his father's shop as a glover's apprentice.

In 1582, the glover's apprentice married Anne Hathaway. Like his father, William married a woman of modest social rank. Anne Hathaway came from a family of established yeomen (small farmers who cultivate their own land), and she had inherited a good sum of money from her father after his death. Anne was eight years older than her husband (she was twenty-six and he was eighteen when they got married). Shakespeare had not achieved his majority (the age at which a boy legally became a man) and was still considered a minor. Because of his status as a minor, and since the wedding could not be completed before Advent (a religious season during which marriages were normally forbidden), a special license had to be secured from the bishop of Worcester. Once this license had been issued on November 27, 1582, William Shakespeare and Anne Hathaway became man and wife.

Six months later it became obvious why the odd marriage had taken place. Anne gave birth to a daughter, Susanna, on May 26, 1583. This means that Anne must have been three months' pregnant at the time William married her. (It is ironic to note that Shakespeare and his wife named their daughter after a biblical character who spurns the sexual advances of a man and maintains her chastity.) Two years later in February 1585, Anne Shakespeare gave birth again, this time to fraternal twins, Hamnet and Judith.

William seems to have regretted his early marriage later in his life, and his plays contain many references that seem to be criticisms of his own youthful misadventures. In *A Midsummer Night's Dream*, Lysander tries to talk his way into Hermia's bed, saying, "One turf shall serve as pillow for us both, / One heart, one bed, two bosoms, and one troth." Hermia turns him away, telling him to "Lie further off, in humane modesty; / Such separation as may well be said / Becomes a virtuous bachelor and a maid."[7] In *Romeo and Juliet* (written at about the same time as *A Midsummer Night's Dream*), Juliet warns against Romeo swearing his love by the moon, saying, "O, swear not by the moon, th' inconstant moon, / That monthly changes in her circled orb, / Lest that thy love prove likewise variable." Juliet then goes on to tell Romeo, "If thy bent of love be honorable, / thy purpose marriage, send me word to-morrow, / By one that I'll procure to come to thee, / Where and what time thou wilt perform the rite."[8] Some critics suggest that the inspiration for *Romeo and Juliet* springs from Shakespeare's hasty marriage to Anne and that the play expresses Shakespeare's disapproval of young love and marriage.

Whatever the case may be for the inspiration of *Romeo and Juliet*, it was generally agreed that William Shakespeare worked as an apprentice in his father's shop until the birth of his twins in 1585. It stands to reason that, faced with a new wife and three hungry mouths to feed, Shakespeare would keep the job he had been employed in since leaving grammar school. However, after 1585, Shakespeare fades from sight until he resurfaces in London in 1592 as the object of a scathing attack by Robert Greene.

Many Shakespeare biographers refer to 1585 to1592 as the "Lost Years." Because of the lack of records, speculation and myth have been quick to step in. Most scholars favor the idea that Shakespeare spent the Lost Years apprenticed to an acting company. Although there is no evidence to support this, it is not beyond belief that a restless William Shakespeare asked a visiting company for employment and that the company, seeing the young man's intelligence and quick wit, agreed to take him on as a hired man or apprentice actor. For Shakespeare, employment with an acting troupe was a step up the economic ladder: The troupes paid better than any other job available to him. There are as many different opinions on how Shakespeare spent the Lost Years as there are scholars to argue them. Various researchers have asserted that he worked as a teacher, a sailor, a soldier, or a lawyer's assistant or that he traveled in Italy (thereby acquiring a knowledge of Italy and Italian culture that shows up in many of his plays, including *Romeo and Juliet*). However Shakespeare spent the Lost Years, one thing is certain: He somehow found his way to London.

The Early Years in London

Shakespeare came to London, as Petruchio says in *The Taming of the Shrew*, on "Such [a] wind as scatters young men through the world / to seek their fortunes farther than at home, / where small experience grows."[9] And indeed, it was in London where William Shakespeare made his fortune. London was a metropolis in more ways than one. It was the home of a thousand entertainments. A person could attend fencing exhibitions, boxing matches (with no gloves), and public executions. For those who favored the violence of animals over the violence of men, there were arenas specializing in bearbaiting (a "sport" where a chained bear fights off a pack of dogs) and cockfights. There were merchants selling everything from apples to yarn, including the latest imports from America and India: tobacco and tea. For people who preferred the sins of the flesh, there were hundreds of taverns and thousands of prostitutes. However, the thing that impressed most travelers to London was not in the city itself but in a field a short distance north of the city walls in an area known as Shoreditch.

It was in Shoreditch that James Burbage, in 1576, built a round, three-story building and named it the Theatre. It was the first time that the word *theatre* had been used in English to refer to a public place for plays. The reason that Burbage had to establish the Theatre outside of the city limits was that actors were thought of as "rouges, vagabonds, and sturdy beggars"[10] who created unrest. Acting troupes had such a bad reputation that they had to have the patronage of nobles in order to avoid persecution. To show their appreciation, the acting companies named themselves after their patrons, such as the Queen's Men or the Lord Chamberlain's Men.

It is thought that around 1589 Shakespeare joined, or somehow became associated with, the combined companies of Lord Strange's Men and the Admiral's Men. Although there are records of his acting, it is unlikely that he was the star actor. At twenty-five years of age he was too old to play female roles (since women were forbidden by law from acting, young boys played female roles) and too old to begin an apprenticeship as an actor. It is likely that he got his start in the theater as a hired man, probably as a "bookkeeper." Like the modern stage manager, it was the job of the bookkeeper to make sure that things ran smoothly during a performance.

The bookkeeper's most important duty was to keep the company's "playbook." Since copyright laws did not exist at the time, each company kept the texts of the plays they performed a secret. It was the bookkeeper's responsibility to buy plays, to get the appropriate license from the Revels Office (the government censor), and to revise the plays according to the actors' criticisms, the troupe's needs, and the government's standards. The bookkeeper also had to copy out the parts for the actors. It is perhaps from experience as a bookkeeper that Shakespeare developed his keen dramatic instinct. And if Shakespeare was indeed a bookkeeper, it is likely that this background, and the added financial opportunity that playwriting offered, led him to compose his own plays. It would allow him to get paid twice: once as a writer and then again as a bookkeeper. Shakespeare the businessman was always on the lookout for extra income.

William Shakespeare's first four history plays (*Henry VI Parts 1, 2,* and *3,* and *Richard III*) made him a force to be

Although he did act in plays, it is unlikely that Shakespeare (kneeling) was the star performer.

reckoned with on the Elizabethan stage. Shakespeare was capitalizing on public opinion. Written between 1589 and 1593, the tetralogy is a celebration of national pride. In 1588, the Spanish Armada had been defeated by Britain despite overwhelming odds. Patriotism in England was at a high, and audiences were thrilled to see the history of their country acted out on the stage.

Shakespeare's theatrical success did not escape the notice of his rival playwrights. Some of the playwrights were enthusiastic about the history plays, but others were not. Rival playwright Robert Greene called Shakespeare an upstart crow, beautified with our feathers, that with his Tygers heart wrapt in a Player's hide, supposes he is as well able to bombast out a blank verse as the best of you: and being an absolute Johannes Factotum [a jack-of-all-trades], is in his own conceit the only Shake-scene in a country.[11]

Greene's anger stems from his belief that Shakespeare, since he lacked a university education, was an inferior writer compared to Greene and his fellow University Wits. Greene believed that university-educated writers were better than "those puppets [actors] . . . that spake from our mouths"[12] and was upset that an outsider like Shakespeare, who was not only undereducated but an actor as well, was being praised by both the nobility and the masses.

Greene's attack had little effect on Shakespeare's growing popularity. He began to write plays at the rate of about two a year. Following the success of his historical tetralogy, Shakespeare expanded his creative horizons beyond dramatizing his country's history. During this period he wrote *Titus Andronicus* and *The Comedy of Errors*, his first tragedy and his first comedy.

The Plague Years 1592–1594

Both *Titus Andronicus* and *The Comedy of Errors* were well received by the public, and things were going smoothly for the budding playwright when disaster struck. From 1592 to 1594, the plague ravished London, killing almost eleven thousand people. In order to combat the plague, people were kept out of confined areas that facilitated the spread of the disease; thus, the public theaters were closed by royal decree. The closing of the public theaters put Shakespeare out of work, and he was forced to earn a living by different means.

In 1593, during the worst of the plague, Shakespeare published his first book. The slim volume contained the poem "Venus and Adonis," an erotic narrative written in the style of Shakespeare's rival Christopher Marlowe. The book was enormously popular, and one biographer noted that "Multitudes bought 'Venus and Adonis'; the poem went through sixteen editions before 1640. No other work by Shakespeare achieved so many printings during this period. Readers thumbed it until it fell to pieces."[13] The sequel to "Venus and Adonis" was published the following year in 1594. Although it never attained the popularity of "Venus and Adonis," "The Rape of Lucrece" nonetheless went on to be reprinted several times before 1640. Although both "Venus and Adonis" and "The Rape of Lucrece" are today considered inferior to his plays, the two poems tell us something about the man writing them. During this period of his life, with the public theaters closed, William Shakespeare tried to make a living by writing poetry calculated to appeal to a select audience: university students, courtiers, lawyers, and, above all, the nobility.

"Venus and Adonis" and "The Rape of Lucrece" were both dedicated to the nineteen-year-old earl of Southampton, Henry Wriothesley. The reason for the dedication was simple: money. With the public theaters closed because of the plague, Shakespeare was effectively out of work as a playwright. By dedicating his "unpolished lines to your Lordship,"[14] Shakespeare was hoping to secure patronage from the young earl. The tradition of patronage was a holdover from the medieval era when artists of all kinds (poets, painters, singers, actors) were

Shakespeare's poems "Venus and Adonis" and "The Rape of Lucrece" were dedicated to Henry Wriothesley (pictured).

dependent on the nobility for their livelihoods. The nobles gave money to the artists in return for performances and works of art.

The relationship between Southampton and William Shakespeare is unclear, but it is certain that Southampton provided Shakespeare with some type of financial assistance during the plague years. Nicholas Rowe tells of

> one instance so singular in the magnificence of this patron of Shakespeare's . . . that my Lord Southampton, at one time, gave him [Shakespeare] a thousand pounds, to enable him to go through with a purchase which he [Southampton] heard he [Shakespeare] had a mind to.[15]

Although the amount here is unrealistic (at the time of his death, Shakespeare's combined holdings were not worth a thousand pounds), there is little doubt that Henry Wriothesley, earl of Southampton, contributed in some way to Shakespeare's livelihood. Scholars believe that Southampton gave Shakespeare the money he needed to buy an interest in the Lord Chamberlain's Men when it re-formed after the plague abated.

At about the same time that Shakespeare wrote and published "Venus and Adonis" and "The Rape of Lucrece," he began work on his famous series of sonnets. Generally, sonnets celebrate the undying love of the poet for his beloved, usually a woman, by listing her beauties and virtues in ornate language. Shakespeare's sonnets are unusual and famous because of their variation on this tradition. *Romeo and Juliet* was especially influenced by Shakespeare's work on the sonnets; the play contains several sonnets and as a whole seems to embody the fragile world of courtly love. There is little doubt among critics and biographers that *Romeo and Juliet*, as well as several other plays, was composed during the plague years with an eye toward the time when the public theaters would reopen.

The Lord Chamberlain's Men

When the plague that had been ravishing London finally loosened its grip on the city in 1594, Shakespeare went back to work. The upper classes, who had fled the deadly city for the healthy countryside, were returning. Everyone from the humblest apprentice to the greatest lord was starving for entertainment after the horror of the plague.

After the plague, Shakespeare bought a share (probably with the money from Southampton) in the re-formed Lord Chamberlain's Men and joined his friends Richard Burbage and William Kemp. Shakespeare became the "ordinary poet" for the Lord Chamberlain's Men, which meant that he was their company playwright. Professional is the best word to describe Shakespeare during this period. Only a few writers during Shakespeare's life were as prolific as he was, especially during 1594–1595. His plays display the poetic skills he developed during the plague while he was writing the sonnets and the poems for Southampton. Shakespeare was beginning to develop the dramatic technique that would reach perfection in his later tragedies and romances.

Four of Shakespeare's comedies were produced during this period: *The Taming of the Shrew*, *The Two Gentlemen of Verona*, *Love's Labor's Lost*, and the fanciful *A Midsummer Night's Dream*. At the same time that Shakespeare was exploring the genre of comedy, he was also writing plays that he knew would sell, such as the histories *King John* and *Richard II*. Shakespeare also produced his second tragedy in this period. *Romeo and Juliet* was hugely successful and continues to be one of his most popular plays after *Hamlet*. *Romeo and Juliet* has been produced onstage more times and in a greater variety of ways than any of Shakespeare's other plays.

Shakespeare's star was on the rise. Shakespeare and the Lord Chamberlain's Men first performed for Queen Elizabeth during the yuletide festivities of 1594. With the deaths of two of Shakespeare's rivals, Christopher Marlowe and Thomas Kyd,

Richard Burbage, Shakespeare's friend and member of the re-formed Lord Chamberlain's Men.

Shakespeare and his acting troupe were in constant demand. In 1596, Shakespeare was awarded a coat of arms from the College of Arms. This had been Shakespeare's life-long dream, and it allowed him to legally sign himself "Gentleman." A gentleman had two primary advantages over a commoner: One, it confirmed class status as a member of the gentry, and two, a gentleman could testify and bring suit in court without taking an oath.

This piece of personal good fortune was marred by the death of Shakespeare's only son, Hamnet, who was buried on August 11, 1596. The death of his son ended any hope Shakespeare may have had for perpetuating the family name and is the reason that no direct descendants of William Shakespeare exist today. In more ways than one, 1596 was a pivotal year in Shakespeare's life.

To reinforce his newly acquired status as a gentleman, Shakespeare bought the biggest house in Stratford-upon-Avon in 1597. It is ironic that as Shakespeare was securing for himself the trappings of a country gentleman in Stratford, he failed to pay his taxes in London. This failure to pay taxes has caused a few scholars to wonder about Shakespeare's financial state, and they believe that his resources were stretched to the limit at this time.

Shakespeare's success in the theater continued in the 1596–1597 season. He produced two works, which coincidently contain two of his most memorable characters. The first was the comedy *The Merchant of Venice*, which contains the character Shylock. The second play was a history called

Henry IV, which contained the character Falstaff. *Henry IV* was such a huge success that it spawned three sequels: *Henry IV Part 2*, *Henry V*, and the comedy *The Merry Wives of Windsor*. Scholars believe that *The Merry Wives of Windsor* was written at the command of Queen Elizabeth, who ordered that the performance be given in front of her and her court during the Garter Feast on St. George's Day, April 23, 1597 (Shakespeare's birthday).

Shakespeare and the Globe

In 1598, William Shakespeare could easily call himself England's most popular playwright. The unparalleled box-office success of his history plays, most notably *Henry IV Parts 1* and *2*, had earned him the praise that other play-wrights only dreamed of. His comedies and tragedies were acclaimed by everyone from Queen Elizabeth down to the humblest apprentice with a penny and an afternoon to spare. This sense of achievement was underscored by Francis Meres, who praised Shakespeare extensively in his book *Palladis Tamia* and compared him to the Greco-Roman playwrights.

The year 1598 came to a dramatic end when the longtime theatrical home of Shakespeare and the Lord Chamberlain's Men, the Theatre, was torn down. Under cover of darkness, a small group gathered at the empty Theatre. The group dismantled the playhouse and carried the timbers through London, then ferried them across the Thames River to Bankside, a district just outside the southern city limits. There, the group reassembled the theater and renamed it the Globe.

The Globe saw the production of some of Shakespeare's best-known plays. It was the first place that the comedies *Much Ado About Nothing, As You Like It, Twelfth Night,* and *All's Well That Ends Well* were performed. It was also the place that saw the inaugural performances of *Julius Caesar* and *Hamlet. Hamlet* is the play that marks the beginning of Shakespeare's great tragedies. It is by far the most recognized of Shakespeare's plays.

Some of Shakespeare's best plays were first performed in the Globe, a recon-struction of which is shown here.

Despite a string of hits, a growing personal fortune, and an increasing recognition of his talent as a playwright, William Shakespeare's life at this point was replete with troubles. His father, John Shakespeare, died in September 1601. Whatever personal grief this may have caused Shakespeare, it paled in comparison to the grief caused by a performance of *Richard II* in February 1601. A group of rebellious nobles (including Shakespeare's friend and patron, the earl of Southampton) was attempting to overthrow Queen Elizabeth. As part of their plan, they paid the Lord Chamberlain's Men to perform *Richard II* in the hope that the play would influence the pop-ulace of London to support their cause. The ploy and the rebellion were complete failures. The rebels were captured by the queen's forces and were quickly executed. A few of the rebels escaped the hangman's noose and were confined to the tower for the rest of Queen Elizabeth's reign, including Shakespeare's friend and patron, Southampton. The investigation after the rebellion cleared the Lord Chamberlain's Men of any intentional wrongdoing. Shakespeare and his fellows breathed a sigh of relief after being cleared by the queen, because if they had been found guilty, their playhouse would have been torn down, their fortunes would have been ruined, and they would have been executed.

The King's Men

The Elizabethan era came to an end on March 24, 1603, when Queen Elizabeth died at the age of seventy. Just before she died, she called her ministers to her and named her successor: "I will that a king succeed me, and who but my kinsman the King of Scots."[16] When James VI of Scotland arrived in London, the reception was muted. The plague was once again ravaging the city (30,561 deaths in one year), and those who could flee the city had already done so. Nonetheless, James VI assumed the throne of England as King James I.

As during previous visitations of the plague, the public theaters were closed, but that did not stop James I from indulging his interest in drama. Within ten days of his arrival in London, James ordered his ministers to issue a royal warrant to the Lord Chamberlain's Men that made the acting company servants of the king. The troupe, out of respect for their new patron, changed the name of the company to the King's Men. The royal warrant testifies to the fact that Shakespeare and the King's Men were the most important acting troupe in existence at that time.

During the reign of James I, acting was not only endorsed as a legitimate profession for Shakespeare and his fellow actors, but was profitable as well. Under James, the rate of pay for court performances was raised from the ten pounds Queen Elizabeth had paid to twenty pounds a performance. In addition, the number of performances at court doubled because both King James and his wife, Queen Anne, were fascinated

The number of plays performed in court doubled during the reign of James I.

by English drama. They wanted to see all the plays they had missed while living in Scotland. Shakespeare and his company were happy to oblige and performed more times at court than all the other London troupes combined. Money flowed into the company's coffers. This was the most profitable time the profession of acting had yet to enjoy.

Between 1603 and 1607, Shakespeare wrote some of his best work. He wrote the comedy *Measure for Measure* to appeal to the new king's interests: justice and mercy. These years also saw the production of Shakespeare's finest tragedies: *Othello*, *King Lear*, *Macbeth*, and *Antony and Cleopatra*. They were in turn followed by the tragedies *Coriolanus* and *Timon of Athens*, which demonstrate a dissatisfaction with the genre of tragedy. In these plays, Shakespeare seems to be groping for something more, something beyond both comedy and tragedy.

In 1608, Shakespeare became a shareholder in the Blackfriars Theatre. Blackfriars was an intimate theater, seating only three hundred people compared with the three thousand that might squeeze into the Globe on any given day. Because seating was limited, ticket prices were higher and the audience was a little more select and sophisticated than the average Globe audience. The success of the Blackfriars Theatre was partly due to the plays that Shakespeare wrote for this new select audience.

Shakespeare wrote neither tragedies, comedies, nor histories but a curious blend of all three genres called "romances." The romances were often Greek stories of love and overwhelming experiences such as quests and shipwrecks. Shakespeare's romances *Pericles* and *Cymbeline* were renowned for their "special effects," such as gods descending from the heavens. These spectacles further increased Shakespeare's celebrity status, and his works, including his sonnets, were openly pirated and sold by booksellers.

Shakespeare's good fortune was not restricted to his professional life; it was also rolling over into his private life as well. Shakespeare's oldest daughter, Susanna, married Dr. John Hall in 1607. A year after the marriage, Shakespeare's first grandchild, Elizabeth Hall, was born. However, later that same year Shakespeare's mother, Mary, died, and she was buried next to her husband in the churchyard at Stratford-upon-Avon.

Back to Stratford

In 1608 or 1609, Shakespeare moved back to Stratford and became a permanent resident who made infrequent trips to

London to see to his theater business and to produce an occasional play. Shakespeare was settling into the role he had been practicing for all his life: the successful country gentleman. After turning his back on the city that made him famous and wealthy, Shakespeare began to take a more active interest in the affairs of his hometown.

Shakespeare was involved in several lawsuits concerning the use of land in the vicinity of Stratford, and he made at least one trip to London for the express purpose of petitioning the Crown to fix the roads between Stratford and London. He was also called to testify in a nasty civil lawsuit concerning an arranged marriage. Shakespeare's testimony in the suit was of little help to either side, and the matter was referred for arbitration.

Shakespeare also kept busy in his semiretirement by writing plays. The period 1610 to 1613 saw the production of three additional romances (*The Winter's Tale*, *The Tempest*, and *The Two Noble Kinsmen*) and one history (*Henry VIII*). After the production of *The Two Noble Kinsmen* in 1613, Shakespeare went into full-time retirement. He may have returned to London on occasion to collect his profits from the Globe and the Blackfriars Theatre, but this is speculation. Nothing is known for sure about Shakespeare again until 1616.

On February 12, 1616, William Shakespeare's younger daughter, Judith, married Thomas Quiney. The marriage was unusual because the groom, a twenty-seven-year-old vintner with a reputation for shadiness, was marrying the thirty-one-year-old daughter of the most famous and richest man in town. Soon after the marriage, a scandal ensued. Thomas Quiney was summoned to court to answer charges of fornication and fathering a child outside of wedlock. What began in February as a joyous time in William Shakespeare's life turned to embarrassment that spring, then to illness, and then, finally, to death.

The circumstances surrounding Shakespeare's month-long illness and eventual death are unclear. Perhaps it resulted from the stress of the scandal of his daughter's marriage and the subsequent court case brought against his son-in-law, or perhaps it was the result of a drinking party. Whatever the cause, William Shakespeare died on April 23, 1616, appropriately enough, the playwright's fifty-second birthday.

The story of William Shakespeare does not end with his death but begins. During his life, Shakespeare published only three poems. However, in 1623, seven years after his death, the first collection of Shakespeare's plays appeared in print. The collection, called the First Folio, was immensely popular and was reprinted four times by 1685. Since that time, Shakespeare's plays have been reprinted thousands of times and have been translated into all the major languages of the world. Shakespeare's impact is still felt today in common words and phrases and in plays, television shows, and movies. Author Alexander Dumas once observed, "After God, only Shakespeare created more."[17]

CHAPTER TWO

The History
of *Romeo*
and *Juliet*

R*omeo and Juliet* is one of the oldest plays still performed for a paying public. It was first performed in London in 1595 and has enjoyed an almost continual presence on the stage since that time. The tragedy of the "star-cross'd lovers" has become an integral part of Western culture; for example, people commonly speak of "would-be Romeos" and laugh when Bugs Bunny, dressed as Juliet, asks, "O Romeo, Romeo, wherefore art thou Romeo?" Even though many people have not seen the play, they are nonetheless familiar with its plot. The same could be said of Shakespeare's original audience.

When Shakespeare's *Romeo and Juliet* premiered more than four hundred years ago, the basic plot of the play was already well established in the audience's minds. The story line and dramatic elements of *Romeo and Juliet* have ancient roots. The plot of the unlucky lovers caught between disputing families goes back to Greek mythology and the legend of Pyramus and Thisbe, who had to court through a crack in a wall. The use of a sleeping potion to avoid an unwelcome marriage can be traced back to the Greek novelist Xenophon in the fourth century A.D. Elements of *Romeo and Juliet* can be found in the literary genre of *Liebestod*, or "love-death." The medieval tale of Tristan and Isolde, an example of the *Liebestod* genre, parallels *Romeo and Juliet* in that the lovers are forced to carry on their affair secretly and the couple dies at the end of the story.

The story of Romeo and Juliet as it is currently known began to take shape in Italy in 1476 when Masuccio of Salerno combined the elements of lovers from warring families with the use of a sleeping potion to avoid an unwelcome marriage. In his work, called *Il Novellino*, Masuccio of Salerno named the lovers Romeo and Giulietta. *Il Novellino* proved to be a popular story, and in 1530 another Italian, Luigi da Porto, retold the story, placing the action in the city of Verona and naming the feuding families the Montecchi and the Cappellati.

Luigi da Porto's story was translated into French by Adrian Sevin in 1542 and adapted as a poem and a play by the Italian writers Clizia and Groto. In 1554, the story of Romeo and Juliet was once again reworked; this time, the Italian writer Bandello turned it into a prose novel, which was subsequently translated into French by Boiastuau in 1559. Boiastuau's version was brought back to England and translated into English by Painter, who includes the story in his book *Palace of Pleasure*, renaming the heroine "Juliet" and calling the families "Capulet" and "Montague." Shakespearean scholars believe that Shakespeare was familiar with *Palace of Pleasure*, but

Fourth-century A.D. *Greek novelist Xenophon.*

33

that he used Arthur Brooke's poem "The Tragical History of Romeus and Juliet" as his primary source. Critic Frank Kermode has said, "To read Brooke with the play in mind is to be struck repeatedly by the easy skill with which Shakespeare has transformed the tale into a dramatic action . . . he obviously had the poem on his desk or in his head."[18]

The Creation of *Romeo and Juliet*

Despite the best efforts of hundreds of researchers, the specifics of Shakespeare's private life remain a mystery. Likewise, scholars know very little about why Shakespeare wrote, what influenced him to compose certain pieces, or what he hoped to achieve with his plays. What is known is based solely on conjecture.

Most Shakespearean scholars agree that *Romeo and Juliet* was probably written between 1592 and 1594. There are three reasons for this belief. The first is that the bubonic plague was ravaging London from June 1592 until June 1594. In an attempt to combat the spread of the disease, Queen Elizabeth outlawed almost all types of public gatherings, including attending the theater. This put Shakespeare out of work and forced him to seek the patronage of Henry Wriothesley, earl of Southampton. It also left him plenty of time to write.

Second, in the year and a half (June 1594 to December 1595) after the ban on theater attendance was lifted, Shakespeare published two poems ("Venus and Adonis" and "The Rape of Lucrece") and put nine different plays on the stage (*The Comedy of Errors, Titus Andronicus, The Taming of the Shrew, The Two Gentlemen of Verona, Love's Labor's Lost, King John, Richard II, Romeo and Juliet,* and *A Midsummer Night's Dream*). This output is remarkable considering the fact that before and after the plague, Shakespeare produced an average of only two plays a year. It is commonly believed that Shakespeare wrote the nine plays while waiting for the theaters to reopen.

The final reason that scholars believe that *Romeo and Juliet* was written during the plague years is the sonnets that are found throughout the play. This has led critics to believe that *Romeo and Juliet* was written at about the same time that Shakespeare was composing his *Sonnets* for Henry Wriothesley, earl of Southampton. The play might be viewed as the embodiment of the world of the love sonnet: a passionate but fragile state that collapses under the weight of reality.

The Performance of *Romeo and Juliet*

The majority of Shakespearean scholars agree that *Romeo and Juliet* was probably first performed in 1595 at the Theatre north of London. Going to see a play in Renaissance England was similar to seeing a play today: How much a person paid determined where the spectator sat. Basic admission was a penny and entitled one to stand in the "yard" that surrounded the stage on three sides. Because these people stood on the ground, they were called "groundlings." Another penny allowed a person to sit in the first tier of wooden seats (cushions were available for rent at the front door), a third penny provided access to the second tier, and a fourth penny the third tier. If a person wanted to splurge, he could rent a private box or sit on the stage while the play was in progress.

However, going to see a play was also quite different in Renaissance England. Acting was far from a respectable profession, and theaters ranked just above bearbaiting dens and brothels. Vendors walked through the audience shouting and selling refreshments during the performance. Prostitutes plied their trade behind the curtains of private boxes. Actors, without the aid of sound amplification, had to shout over the noise to be heard. If the audience did not like the play, they would shout at the actors and throw things (like tomatoes, which were sold for that express purpose).

Acting was strictly a male profession in Renaissance England. Female actors were considered to be lewd and were forbidden by law from appearing on the stage, so young boys played the female roles. Likewise, "respectable" women did not attend the public theater, but many of them did attend disguised as men. The public theater was also used as a rendezvous for people having extramarital affairs.

It is into this circuslike atmosphere that Shakespeare introduced *Romeo and Juliet*. It is impossible to know for sure how a Renaissance audience would have responded to the play. They would have cheered during the play's fight scenes, but did they talk during the balcony scene? Or, like modern audiences, were they hushed into silence by the scene's tender feelings?

Although *Romeo and Juliet* has always enjoyed popularity with the masses, its merits are debated among critics. Francis Meres, writing in 1598, compared Shakespeare to the ancient

In Renaissance England, groundings, members of an audience who stood in the yard that surrounded the stage on three sides, could watch a play for a penny.

Greek dramatists: "As Plautus and Seneca are accounted the best for Comedy and Tragedy among the Latins: so Shakespeare among the English is the most excellent in both kinds for the stage . . . witness his . . . *Romeo and Juliet.*"[19] How-ever, not all of Shakespeare's contemporaries were as enthralled with him as Francis Meres.

Ben Jonson, a fellow playwright whom Shakespeare helped professionally, admired Shakespeare, but said, "Many times [Shakespeare] fell into those things [made obvious mistakes] [that] could not escape laughter."[20] John Dryden, writing in 1679, praised Shakespeare for understanding the nature of passion but faulted Shakespeare for his language, observing that "he often obscures his meaning by his

Seventeenth-century writer John Dryden praised Shakespeare's passion but claimed that his language was sometimes "unintelligible."

words, and sometimes makes it unintelligible."[21] Frank Kermode observes that critics throughout the centuries have admired *Romeo and Juliet* "for its pathetic rather than for its tragic power; and many would agree with [Samuel] Johnson that in this instance . . . Shakespeare's 'pathetic strains are . . . polluted with some unexpected depravation.'"[22] In other words, the play has been attacked because it falls short of the catastrophic perfection that can be found in Shakespeare's later tragedies such as *Hamlet, Julius Caesar*, and *Macbeth*.

What Was Shakespeare Trying to Achieve?

The question that usually arises when one is studying Shakespeare's plays is "What was Shakespeare trying to achieve?" Although the answer to this question is pure conjecture, it is safe to assume that Shakespeare wanted to demonstrate that he was capable of writing more than just comedies and histories. Until the creation of *Romeo and Juliet*, Shakespeare was famous for these types of plays, and in an attempt to "branch out," he began to compose tragedies.

Shakespeare's first tragedy, *Titus Andronicus*, was popular with audiences not because of the dramatic intensity of its dialogue but because it was a blood-spurting, "hack-and-slash" thriller. The play was so bad that by the end of the seventeenth century it was blasted as a "heap of rubbish,"[23] and some tried to prove that Shakespeare had not written it. *Romeo and Juliet*, Shakespeare's second tragedy, can be viewed as Shakespeare's attempt to combine a "hack-and-slash" thriller and dramatically moving dialogue into a true tragedy that avoids the sensationalism of *Titus Andronicus*.

Romeo and Juliet also represents another step in Shakespeare's slow expansion of the "classical unities." The "classical unities," based on Greek and Roman drama, dictated that the action of the play should take place in a single location, a play should have a single plot, and the plot should be resolved within a single day. Shakespeare had begun to chip away at this idea with his history plays, in which the playwright asked the audience to accept the revolutionary concept that the stage could be England in one scene and France in the next. *Romeo and Juliet* violates the unity of both time and location: The action of the play takes place over three days, and a small part of the play takes place in Mantua.

Shakespeare probably needed to alter the classical unities to accommodate an expanded sense of drama. This expanded sense of drama is evident in the "tragedy" of *Romeo and Juliet*. The hero of a tragedy is marked by an obvious character flaw such as jealousy, selfishness, or vanity that leads to his downfall. However, Romeo and Juliet seem to lack any type of tragic flaw, and their downfall is the result of the negligence of a second party.

Shakespeare was also attempting to incorporate some of the poetics from his *Sonnets* into the dramatic poetry of *Romeo and Juliet*. The play contains several complete sonnets—one is the prologue and a second is when Romeo and Juliet first meet (I.v.93–106). The play also shares language and images with the *Sonnets*. For instance, in several poems the narrator of the *Sonnets* speaks of his unrequited love for a Dark Lady. When Romeo first appears on the stage, he is unhappy about his love affair with the dark-haired Rosaline, and he laments his luck in language typical of courtly lovers.

Shakespeare's ultimate goal as a playwright was the same as that of any playwright: to write a play that people would pay to see. This was at no time more important to Shakespeare than during the years immediately following the plague. The closure of the public theaters in London from 1592 to 1594 had undoubtedly hurt Shakespeare financially, and when the theaters reopened, Shakespeare needed to make money. Many of the plays that came out of this period of his life remain popular favorites, and *Romeo and Juliet* is the most beloved of these plays.

It is difficult to say for certain how Shakespeare's audience reacted to *The Tragedy of Romeo and Juliet*. In 1598, Francis Meres praised the play and compared Shakespeare to the Roman playwrights Plautus and Seneca. However, in 1662 Samuel Pepys blasted the play as "the worst acted that ever I saw."[24] One thing that is certain is that *Romeo and Juliet* has withstood the test of time and has been performed thousands of times in the four hundred years since Shakespeare first penned it. *Romeo and Juliet* has been performed as an opera, a ballet, and a Broadway musical; and has been turned into several popular movies. The timeless appeal of the play can be traced to at least two elements: its action and the story of two young lovers fighting the world to be together. It's a story that is as old as the world but as fresh as the teenage love that it portrays.

CHAPTER THREE

The Plot of
Romeo
and Juliet

L ike all of Shakespeare's plays, *The Tragedy of Romeo and Juliet* is filled with memorable characters. Romeo and Juliet are the two lovers from the feuding Montague and Capulet families, respectively. Mercutio and Benvolio are friends of Romeo (Mercutio is also a kinsman to Escalus, the prince of Verona), while the Nurse serves as Juliet's confidant. Paris is a young nobleman (who is related to Escalus) attempting to win Juliet's heart and is favored by her parents. Tybalt is a master swordsman from the Capulet family who kills Mercutio and is in turn killed by Romeo. Friar Lawrence is the priest who marries Romeo and Juliet in secret with the hope that their union will bring peace to the feuding families. Friar Lawrence is also responsible for encouraging Juliet to drink the sleeping potion that forces the play toward its tragic conclusion.

The Tragedy of Romeo and Juliet begins with a prologue that provides a brief history of the feud between the Capulets and the Montagues as well as an outline of the play's events. Aside from previewing the plot of the play, the prologue is interesting for two other reasons. First, the prologue is spoken by a "Chorus." The Chorus is a holdover from the classical plays of the Greeks and was used by Greek dramatists to symbolize the voice of reason and to comment on the action of the play. *Romeo and Juliet* is unique because it is the only tragedy in which Shakespeare uses a Chorus. It seems Shakespeare had mixed feelings about the Chorus as a dramatic device: Although the Chorus opens acts 1 and 2, Shakespeare fails to use it for the final three acts. The second thing that is interesting about the prologue is that it introduces the sonnet form into the play. A sonnet is a fourteen-line poem written in iambic pentameter. Shakespeare used what is called the "Shakespearean" sonnet form (he did not invent it but was its most famous practitioner), which has the rhyme scheme ABAB-CDCD-EFEF-GG.

Act 1, Scene 1: Street Brawl

Romeo and Juliet, like many of Shakespeare's plays, begins *in medias res* (Latin for "in the middle of things"). Two servants from the house of Capulet meet two of Montague's servants on the street, and the two groups of men begin trading insults. Benvolio enters and tries to make peace, but he is followed by Tybalt, who challenges Benvolio: "What, art thou drawn among these heartless hinds? / Turn thee, Benvolio, look upon thy death."[25] The two groups of men begin to fight and are in turn attacked by an angry mob of citizens who, irritated by the continual feuding, shout, "Down with the Capulets! Down with the Montagues!"[26] Following on the heels of the citizens are the heads of both families and their wives. The two old men, Montague and Capulet, attempt to fight but are restrained by their wives.

Finally, the Prince of Verona arrives on the scene with his train and calms things down. He admonishes both the Capulets and the Montagues for disturbing the peace of the city with their brawls and forbids them from doing so again under penalty of death. He then separates the warring factions like children, commanding Capulet to accompany him and telling Montague that he will speak with him that afternoon.

While trying to pacify the servants of Capulet and Montague, Benvolio (right) is challenged by Tybalt (left).

After the Prince leaves with Capulet, Montague turns to Benvolio and asks him how the fight started. Benvolio explains and the conversation drifts to the whereabouts of Montague's son, Romeo. Benvolio reports that he saw Romeo earlier that morning before the sun had risen walking in a sycamore grove west of the city and that Romeo fled when Benvolio tried to approach him. Montague, like a caring father, expresses concern for his son's well-being and asks Benvolio to try to find out the cause of Romeo's distress. As Romeo enters, Montague and Lady Montague exit so that Benvolio may question Romeo.

Benvolio asks, "What sadness lengthens Romeo's hours?"[27] and Romeo replies that the woman with whom he is in love does not love him. Romeo then goes on to lament his unrequited love in language appropriate to a courtly lover: "Love is a smoke made with the fume of sighs, / Being purg'd, a fire sparkling in lover's eyes, / Being vex'd, a sea nourish'd with loving tears, / A choking gall, and a preserving sweet."[28] Romeo then asks Benvolio how to get over this failed love affair and Benvolio suggests, "Examine other beauties."[29] Romeo doubts that courting other women will ease his pain, but Benvolio promises that it will work.

Act 1, Scene 2: Invitation to a Party

The action of the play then shifts to Capulet, who is talking with Paris on a Verona street. Paris asks Capulet for Juliet's hand in marriage, but Capulet puts him off, claiming, "My child is yet a stranger in the world, / She hath not seen the change of fourteen years; / Let two more summers wither in their pride, / Ere we may think her ripe to be a bride."[30] Paris reminds Capulet that women younger than Juliet are already mothers, but Capulet shrugs off the remark and advises Paris that once he wins Juliet's love, Capulet will consent to the marriage. Capulet then invites Paris to a feast at his house so that he may have the opportunity to court Juliet and win her heart. Capulet gives a list of guests to a servant and asks the servant to seek the guests out and invite them to the feast.

However, the servant cannot read and stops the first two people he sees walking in the street to read the list to him: Benvolio and Romeo. Romeo reads the list to the servant and learns that his would-be lover, Rosaline, has been asked to attend the Capulets' feast. Benvolio suggests that he and Romeo attend the feast so that Romeo can compare Rosaline to other women, with the hope that he will see that Rosaline is not a "swan" but a "crow."[31] Romeo doubts that it will work but agrees to go along anyway.

Act 1, Scene 3: Lady Capulet and the Nurse

The scene then shifts to the Capulets' house where Lady Capulet and the Nurse are searching for Juliet. Lady Capulet has important news for Juliet and at first she sends the Nurse away so that she and Juliet may speak in private, but then calls the Nurse back. When Lady Capulet asks the Nurse how old Juliet is, the Nurse answers the question and then launches into a bawdy anecdote about Juliet's younger years. Lady Capulet finally silences the Nurse and asks Juliet what she thinks about marriage. Juliet replies that she has not given much thought to marriage. Lady Capulet then tells Juliet that Paris wants Juliet for his wife, and she extols Paris's many virtues. Juliet, wanting to be a dutiful daughter, replies, "I'll look to like, if looking liking move; / But no more deep will I endart mine eye / Than your consent gives strength to make it fly."[32] The conversation is interrupted by a servant who informs Lady Capulet that guests are arriving; all three women exit to attend the feast.

Act 1, Scene 4: Queen Mab

The next scene takes place in front of the Capulets' house as Romeo, Benvolio, and Mercutio prepare to attend the feast. Mercutio and Benvolio are teasing Romeo about being lovesick. Romeo is unmoved by their joking and says that attending the feast is not wise. When Mercutio asks why, Romeo replies that he had a dream, but before he can describe the dream Mercutio replies that "dreamers often lie"[33] and launches into the Queen Mab soliloquy, which is often praised as one of Shakespeare's greatest dramatic speeches. The soliloquy describes in detail Queen Mab ("the fairies' midwife"), her chariot ("an empty hazelnut"), her driver ("a small grey-coated gnat"[34]), and her night rides, which cause men and women to dream. Mercutio ends by dismissing dreams as "the children of an idle brain,"[35] but Romeo is still anxious about attending the feast: "I fear, too early, for my mind misgives / Some consequence yet hanging in the stars / Shall bitterly begin his fearful date / With this night's revels."[36] Despite his misgivings, Romeo still accompanies his friends to the feast.

Act 1, Scene 5: Romeo and Juliet Meet

Inside the Capulet home, the feast is in full swing: Servants are scurrying about with dishes and drinks, musicians are playing, people are dancing, and Capulet is busy greeting his guests. While his friends are cavorting about the dance floor, Romeo sees Juliet for the first time and falls instantly in love: "Did my heart love till now? Forswear it, sight! / For I ne'er saw true beauty till this night."[37] Since nobody seems to know her name, Romeo decides to approach her.

Meanwhile, Tybalt has recognized Romeo and reports his presence to Capulet: "Uncle, this is a Montague, our foe; / A villain that is hither come in spite / To scorn at our solemnity this night."[38] Capulet, who is feeling generous, tells Tybalt to leave Romeo alone and that Romeo is welcome as long as he behaves himself. Tybalt insists that something must be done because it's a shame for them to let their mortal enemy remain within the house. Capulet, irritated by Tybalt's insistence, humiliates Tybalt publicly to remind him who the master of the house is. Tybalt, injured by the twin insults of Romeo's presence and Capulet's rebuke, swears revenge: "I will withdraw, but this intrusion shall, / Now seeming sweet, convert to bitt'rest gall."[39]

Across the room, Romeo touches Juliet's hand and speaks to her for the first time as they dance. The couple's first conversation takes the form of a sonnet with an extra couplet at the end. The lines of the sonnet are almost equally divided between Romeo and Juliet (Romeo has one line more than Juliet). Romeo asks forgiveness for touching Juliet's hand, compares his lips to pilgrims waiting to kiss a saint, and offers to kiss any wrong away. Juliet tells Romeo that "you do wrong your hand too much"[40] and that it is appropriate for pilgrims to kiss the hands of saints. Romeo then suggests that lips should be pressed together like palms in prayer and he kisses Juliet. Juliet protests and Romeo quickly removes the kiss by kissing it away.

The lovers' flirtation is interrupted by the Nurse, who informs Juliet that her mother is looking for her. Romeo asks the Nurse who Juliet's mother is and the Nurse tells him that Juliet's mother is Lady Capulet. Before Romeo can react, his friend Benvolio appears at his side and whisks him away because the feast is about to break up. As the guests leave, Juliet asks her Nurse who Romeo is and the Nurse tells her that Romeo is a Montague. Juliet replies, "My only love sprung from my only hate! / Too early seen unknown, and known too late! / Prodigious birth of love it is to me / That I must love a loathed enemy."[41]

At a dance inside the Capulet home, Romeo encounters Juliet for the first time and flirtatiously touches her hand.

Act 2, Scene 1: The Capulets' Orchard

Act 2 begins with the Chorus commenting on the blooming love between Romeo and Juliet. The Chorus points out that, even though circumstances are against the lovers, "passion lends them power, time means, to meet, / Temp'ring extremities with extreme sweet."[42] The Chorus foreshadows the "balcony scene" that will occur later in this act when Romeo courts Juliet as she stands on a balcony outside of her room.

The action of the play begins with Romeo deciding to stay at the Capulets' house, where he hopes to catch a glimpse of Juliet through a window. When Benvolio and Mercutio approach, looking for Romeo, Romeo hides. Benvolio and Mercutio call out for Romeo, but Romeo ignores their calls, even when Mercutio begins to mock him. Benvolio and Mercutio call off their search when they realize that it is futile.

Act 2, Scene 2: The Balcony

After Benvolio and Mercutio leave, Romeo sees a light in a window and hopes that it is Juliet. Romeo then compares Juliet to the sun and claims that she is brighter and more beautiful than any heavenly body. This soliloquy by Romeo begins one of the most well-known scenes in drama—the balcony scene between Romeo and Juliet. The scene is so recognizable that even people who have never seen the play are familiar with it.

Juliet appears on the balcony and asks, "O Romeo, Romeo, wherefore art thou Romeo? / Deny thy father and refuse thy name; / Or, if thou wilt not, be but my sworn love, / and I'll no longer be a Capulet."[43] Unknown to her, Romeo is hiding in the garden and overhears her talking to herself and decides to listen a bit longer. Juliet continues to talk to herself, discussing the nature of names. She decides that names have no meaning and that if Romeo were not Romeo she would still love him.

At this point, Romeo interrupts Juliet's musings and startles her. Juliet demands to know who is hiding in the bushes listening to her. Romeo identifies himself and Juliet, although

Actors perform the famous balcony scene between Romeo and Juliet at an open air theater in London.

pleased to see Romeo, warns him to leave the garden before he is discovered by her kinsmen, who will surely kill him. Romeo declares that he would gladly face death rather than live his life without Juliet's love. Juliet declares her love for Romeo and then asks if he loves her. Romeo begins to swear his love by the moon, but Juliet stops him: "O, swear not by the moon, th' inconstant moon, / That monthly changes in her circled orb, / Lest that thy love prove likewise variable."[44] Romeo asks what he should swear by, and Juliet tells him to swear by himself. She then changes the direction of the conversation and tells Romeo that he should leave:

Although I joy in thee,

I have no joy of this contract to-night,

It is too rash, too unadvis'd, too sudden,

Too like the lightning, which doth cease to be

Ere one can say it lightens.[45]

Romeo stops Juliet as she leaves and asks if she will give him a vow of love. Juliet reminds him that she gave him such a vow earlier but that she would be more than happy to give it again. The Nurse begins to call for Juliet, and Juliet tells Romeo to wait for a moment while she goes to see what the Nurse wants. When Juliet reappears on the balcony, she tells Romeo,

If that thy bent of love be honorable,

Thy purpose marriage, send me word to-morrow,

By one that I'll procure to come to thee,

Where and what time thou wilt perform the rite,

And all my fortunes at thy foot I'll lay,

And follow thee my lord throughout the world.[46]

As the Nurse calls Juliet again, Romeo promises that he will send Juliet word on the following day about when and where the marriage will take place. Juliet exits the balcony and then returns again to exchange vows with Romeo once more. As Juliet leaves the balcony one final time, she utters the immortal phrase "Good night, good night! Parting is such sweet sorrow, / that I shall say good night till it be morrow."[47]

Act 2, Scene 3: Friar Lawrence's Cell

The next scene opens with Friar Lawrence tending his plants and wondering aloud at their nature and variety. Friar Lawrence ponders the paradox that "Within the infant rind of this weak flower / Poison hath residence and medicine power,"[48] which can be seen as a metaphor for the troubled relationship between Romeo and Juliet. Although their love is young and beautiful, it still has the power to poison as well as heal.

Romeo enters and greets Friar Lawrence, who, noticing that Romeo has been up all night, thinks that he has been with

Rosaline. Romeo corrects the priest and tells Friar Lawrence that "I have been feasting with my enemy" and that "my heart's dear love is set / On the fair daughter of rich Capulet,"[49] whom he wishes to marry. Friar Lawrence is happy that Romeo is over Rosaline, but he criticizes him for so quickly falling out of love with one woman and into love with another. Despite his criticisms, Friar Lawrence agrees to marry Romeo and Juliet.

Act 2, Scene 4: Teasing the Nurse

The scene opens with Benvolio and Mercutio wondering where Romeo has been all night. Benvolio reveals that Tybalt has sent a letter to Romeo challenging him to a duel. The two men then pun on Tybalt's name and praise his swordsmanship in a teasing manner. Romeo enters and Mercutio begins to tease Romeo about giving the slip to his friends the night before. Romeo, elated because he is in love with Juliet, responds to Mercutio in kind and the two men banter.

The Nurse and her man Peter approach the three jesting men and ask for Romeo. Mercutio calls the Nurse ugly and refers to her as a prostitute, but the Nurse, although shocked by Mercutio's behavior, refuses to indulge in name-calling with him. Romeo identifies himself to the Nurse, who says she must speak to him in private. Romeo then excuses himself from his friends and promises to meet them later at his father's house.

When they are alone, the Nurse rebukes Romeo for letting Mercutio speak to her in such a manner. She then goes on to warn Romeo that he should be honest in his dealings with Juliet because she is a naive young woman. Romeo assures the Nurse that his intentions are honorable and that Juliet should come to Friar Lawrence's cell in the afternoon on the pretext of making a confession so that the priest can marry them. Romeo also gives the Nurse a rope ladder so that he may climb into Juliet's room later that night to consummate the marriage. The scene ends with Romeo asking the Nurse to praise him to Juliet and the Nurse agreeing to do so.

Act 2, Scene 5: Preparing for the Secret Marriage

The action of the play then shifts from the streets of Verona to an orchard near the Capulet house where Juliet is anxiously awaiting her Nurse. The Nurse finally appears and delays giving Juliet the news. The more that Juliet begs for news of Romeo, the more unwilling the Nurse is to speak of it. Finally, the Nurse tells Juliet that Romeo has arranged for them to be married that afternoon in Friar Lawrence's cell and that Romeo has provided a rope ladder so that he may climb up to Juliet's window later that night.

Act 2, Scene 6: A Few Moments Before the Ceremony

In the next scene, Friar Lawrence is expressing his concerns to Romeo about the impending marriage. Romeo dismisses the priest's worries and expresses the happiness that he feels whenever he sees Juliet. Friar Lawrence is not soothed by Romeo's words and advises the young man that "The sweetest honey / Is loathsome in his own deliciousness, / And in the taste confounds the appetite. / Therefore love moderately: long love doth so; / Too swift arrives as tardy as too slow."[50] Juliet arrives and the two lovers see each other in the daylight for the first and only time. The scene ends as Friar Lawrence leads Romeo and Juliet away to marry them.

Act 3, Scene 1: The Deaths of Mercutio and Tybalt

The first scene of act 3 represents the dramatic climax of *Romeo and Juliet*. It begins with Benvolio telling Mercutio, "let's retire, / The day is hot, the Capels are abroad / And if we meet we shall not scape a brawl, / For now, these hot days, is the mad blood stirring."[51] Mercutio responds by telling Benvolio that the weather is not the problem, it is Benvolio's own quarrelsome nature. As Mercutio and Benvolio argue about who is the most quarrelsome between them, Tybalt and members of the Capulet household approach them. Tybalt attempts to ask them where Romeo is, and Mercutio replies with insults while Benvolio pleads with both Mercutio and Tybalt to control their tempers while in public.

Unfortunately, Romeo enters the scene and Tybalt, seeing Romeo, forgets about Mercutio and challenges Romeo to a fight. Romeo, not wanting to fight Juliet's cousin, turns down Tybalt's challenge:

I do protest that I never injured thee,

But love thee better than thou canst devise,

Till thou shalt know the reason of my love,

And so, good Capulet—which name I tender

As dearly as my own—be satisfied.[52]

However, Mercutio, feeling that Romeo is being dishonorable by not answering Tybalt's challenge, offers to fight Tybalt to defend his friend's honor. Romeo attempts to stop Mercutio and Tybalt from fighting by stepping between them. Tybalt seizes the opportunity and manages to stab Mercutio under Romeo's arm, then runs away. As Mercutio dies, he pronounces a curse: "A plague a' both your houses! / They have made worms' meat of me."[53]

When Tybalt returns, Romeo is beside himself with rage. He challenges Tybalt:

Now, Tybalt, take the "villain" back again

That late thou gavest me, for Mercutio's soul

Is but a little way above our heads,

Staying for thine to keep him company.

Either thou or I, or both, must go with him.[54]

Tybalt accepts Romeo's challenge and the two men fight. Romeo stabs Tybalt and Tybalt falls. Benvolio, only realizing part of the tragedy, encourages Romeo to flee. Romeo, realizing that he has just ruined any chance he and Juliet had for happiness, exclaims, "O, I am fortune's fool!"[55] and runs away.

Soon after Romeo has fled the scene, the citizens of Verona arrive, followed by the Prince, Montague, Capulet, and their wives. The Prince asks Benvolio what happened, and Benvolio relates the tale of the fight between Tybalt and Mercutio, and then the fight between Tybalt and Romeo. Lady Capulet accuses Benvolio of lying to protect Romeo, and Montague defends his son by pointing out that Romeo was Mercutio's friend and that he was in the right to kill Tybalt. The Prince silences both the Capulets and the Montagues by saying that both families are responsible for the death of his kinsman Mercutio and that he intends to fine both parties. He further pronounces Romeo's banishment from Verona and threatens to kill him if he returns.

Act 3, Scene 2: Juliet Learns of her Kinsman's Death

Meanwhile at the Capulet home, Juliet is unaware that her husband has just killed her cousin. Instead, she is thinking about the joys of the wedding night and anxiously awaiting Romeo. The Nurse enters and Juliet asks her for news of Romeo. The Nurse, visibly upset, garbles the story of the fight between Romeo and Tybalt, and Juliet thinks that Romeo is dead. The Nurse finally gets the story straight and tells Juliet that Romeo has killed Tybalt and as a result, has been banished by the Prince. Juliet laments that somebody as handsome as Romeo could actually be such a cold-blooded killer, but when the Nurse wishes shame on Romeo, Juliet comes to her husband's defense: "Blister'd be thy tongue! / for such a wish! He was not born to shame: / Upon his brow shame is asham'd to sit."[56] Juliet then resolves to stand by her husband despite the injury he has done to her, although she believes that she will never see him again and that "death, not Romeo, take my maidenhead!"[57] The Nurse consoles Juliet by telling her that she will find Romeo and bring him back to comfort her.

Act 3, Scene 3: Plotting an Escape

The next scene opens with Friar Lawrence informing Romeo that the Prince has banished him for killing Tybalt. The priest points out that the Prince could have sentenced Romeo to death but has instead been merciful and merely exiled him. Romeo replies, "'Tis torture and not mercy. Heaven is here / Where Juliet lives, and every cat and dog / And little mouse, every unworthy thing, / Live here in heaven and may look on her, / But Romeo may not."[58] Friar Lawrence tries to reason with Romeo, but Romeo will not listen.

A knock on the door interrupts their argument and the Nurse enters. The Nurse tells Romeo that Juliet is beside herself with grief and is calling out for him. Romeo tries to stab himself with a dagger but is stopped by the Nurse. Friar Lawrence, shocked by Romeo's behavior, rebukes Romeo:

Hold thy desperate hand!

Art thou a man? Thy form cries out thou art;

Thy tears are womanish, thy wild acts denote

The unreasonable fury of a beast.

Unseemly woman in a seeming man,

And ill-beseeming beast in seeming both,

Thou hast amaz'd me![59]

The priest then reminds Romeo of his duties as a man and recounts for him all the happiness that lies before him. He tells Romeo to go to Juliet and in the morning to escape to Mantua while Friar Lawrence begs the Prince to allow Romeo to return. Romeo, brought to his senses by the priest's impassioned speech, agrees to visit Juliet that night and to flee to Mantua in the morning as Friar Lawrence suggests.

Act 3, Scene 4: Capulet Decides to Marry Juliet to Paris

Meanwhile, Capulet is speaking with Paris about the events of the day. Capulet suddenly tells Paris that he thinks Juliet will marry him if he orders her to. He tells Paris that he should prepare to marry Juliet on Thursday, and then he tells Lady Capulet to tell Juliet the news.

Act 3, Scene 5: The Lovers Part

In the morning, Romeo and Juliet appear at Juliet's window as Romeo is preparing to leave. Juliet begs Romeo not to leave and tells him that it is not yet morning, but still night. Romeo, knowing that it is morning, replies that he must leave or die. Juliet insists that it is not morning and Romeo relents and agrees to stay even if it means his death. Juliet quickly changes her mind and tells Romeo that he must hurry and leave for Mantua before he is captured by the Prince's guards.

The Nurse suddenly enters and tells Juliet that her mother is on her way to Juliet's room. Romeo climbs down the rope ladder and bids Juliet farewell. Juliet asks if they will ever meet again and Romeo replies, "I doubt it not, and all these woes shall serve / For sweet discourses in our times to come."[60] Juliet is not so optimistic and tells Romeo, "Methinks I see thee now, thou art so low, / As one dead in the bottom of a tomb."[61] Romeo responds by attempting to comfort Juliet one more time before he leaves.

After Romeo has left, Lady Capulet enters Juliet's room and asks her how she is feeling. Juliet responds that she is not feeling well because of the loss of Tybalt, and Lady Capulet attempts to make Juliet feel better by telling her that she is going to send an assassin to Mantua to kill Romeo. Juliet feigns happiness at the news, which encourages Lady Capulet to tell Juliet that her father has arranged for her to marry Paris on Thursday. Juliet, shocked by the news and now caught in a quandary, tells her mother that she is not yet ready to marry.

At that moment Capulet enters and asks why Juliet is still crying. Lady Capulet tells him that Juliet does not want to marry Paris. Capulet is at first confused by the news, but when he does understand he flies into a rage. He calls Juliet "you green sickness carrion," "young baggage," and a "disobedient wretch."[62] Capulet then complains to his wife, "Wife, we scarce thought us blest / That God had lent us but this only child, / But now I see this one is one too much, / And that we have a curse in having her."[63] Lady Capulet and the Nurse try to calm Capulet down, but he continues to insult and deride Juliet. Before Capulet storms out of the room he tells Juliet that she will marry Paris or "die in the streets."[64]

Juliet, unsure of what to do, asks the Nurse for guidance. The Nurse suggests that Juliet marry Paris to appease her father since Romeo has been banished and nobody (except for herself and Friar Lawrence) knows that she and Romeo are married. At first Juliet seems to accept the Nurse's advice and tells the Nurse to tell her parents that she has gone to Friar Lawrence to seek absolution for her sins. After the Nurse leaves, Juliet curses the Nurse for her advice and plans to visit Friar Lawrence to see if he can help her out of this difficult situation.

Act 4, Scene 1: Plans for a Faked Death

Act 4 of *Romeo and Juliet* begins with Paris speaking with Friar Lawrence and making arrangements for his marriage to Juliet. Friar Lawrence voices his concerns about the marriage, but Paris insists that it is the only way to cure Juliet of her grief for Tybalt. Juliet enters in the middle of their conversation and Paris greets her as "my lady, and my wife."[65] Paris and Juliet then engage in a conversation in which Juliet intentionally misleads Paris about her feelings and the reason why she is visiting Friar Lawrence.

After Paris leaves, Juliet pleads with Friar Lawrence for help, saying that she would rather kill herself than marry Paris. The priest attempts to calm Juliet by telling her that she can avoid the marriage to Paris by drinking a potion he has prepared that will make it look like she's dead, and after forty-two hours she will awake as if "from a pleasant sleep."[66] Friar Lawrence further

Romeo, banished for killing Tybalt, reluctantly parts with Juliet.

explains that he will write a letter to Romeo in Mantua and inform him of their plan so that Romeo does not mistakenly believe that Juliet has actually died. Juliet agrees to the plan, takes the potion, and leaves.

Act 4, Scene 2: Acknowledging Her Father's Will

The action of the play then shifts back to the Capulet house where the servants are busy preparing for the wedding. Juliet enters and kneels down before her father and asks his forgiveness, saying, "Henceforward I am ever rul'd by you."[67] Her father is pleased to hear this and orders that the wedding take place the very next morning rather than on Thursday. Juliet takes this news calmly and excuses herself to prepare for the ceremony.

Act 4, Scene 3: Juliet Drinks the Sleeping Potion

After Juliet has prepared for the marriage and after her mother and the Nurse have left the room, she takes out a dagger and Friar Lawrence's potion. Juliet wonders aloud if the plan will work or whether she will awake in the morning and be forced to marry Paris. Her thoughts then shift to Friar Lawrence, and she wonders if the priest is giving her poison to cover his own mistake. Juliet then dwells on the macabre vision of waking up in the tomb before Romeo has rescued her and fighting with Tybalt's ghost. Finally, she drinks the potion and falls upon her bed.

Act 4, Scene 5: The Sleeping Juliet Is Discovered

In the morning, the Nurse and Lady Capulet attempt to wake Juliet, but fail. Capulet enters, asking for the cause of the delay, and both women tell him that Juliet is dead. Capulet checks his daughter and proclaims, "Out alas, she's cold, / Her blood is settled, and her joints are stiff; / Life and these lips have long been separated."[68] Friar Lawrence and Paris enter soon after and learn that Juliet has died. Paris, beside himself with grief, curses his luck. Friar Lawrence, aware that Juliet is only in a deep slumber and wanting things to go as planned, offers soothing words to the Capulets, the Nurse, and Paris but insists on a quick burial for Juliet. The scene ends with the characters leaving the stage one by one, and Peter, the Nurse's man, dismissing the musicians in a comic fashion.

Act 5, Scene 1: Romeo Receives Tragic News

The final act of *Romeo and Juliet* begins on the streets of Mantua where Romeo is pondering the meaning of a dream that left him feeling some "joyful news at hand."[69] Romeo dreamed that Juliet found him dead, and by kissing him, breathed life back into him. Romeo is approached by Balthasar, a Montague servant, who tells him that Juliet is dead. Romeo, overwhelmed by heartache, orders his servant to hire some horses and prepare to ride for Verona. Balthasar begs Romeo, saying, "I do beseech you, sir, have patience. / Your looks are pale and wild, and do import / Some misadventure,"[70] but Romeo will not wait and vows, "Juliet, I will lie with thee to-night."[71] Romeo then seeks out an apothecary (a pharmacist), who reluctantly sells him poison.

Act 5, Scene 2: Friar Lawrence Recognizes the Mistake

The action then shifts to Friar Lawrence's cell in Verona, where Friar Lawrence greets Friar John (the priest that Friar Lawrence had given the letter to explaining the situation) and asks about Romeo. Friar John replies that he was unable to deliver the letter because he was quarantined after visiting a sick friend. Friar Lawrence quickly realizes that he must go to Juliet's tomb to prevent a disaster.

Act 5, Scene 3: In the Capulet Family Tomb

The final scene of *Romeo and Juliet* begins with Paris entering the Capulet family crypt. Paris orders his page to stand watch outside and whistle if anybody approaches. Paris begins to put flowers around Juliet's tomb, grieving for her death and his loss. The page whistles and Paris decides to hide in order to discover who is approaching. Balthasar and Romeo enter the crypt. Romeo dismisses Balthasar and begins to pry open Juliet's tomb so that he may die next to his beloved.

Paris watches this from hiding and thinks,

This is that banish'd haughty Montague,

That murd'red my love's cousin, with which grief

It is supposed the fair creature died,

And here is come to do some villainous shame

To the dead bodies. I will apprehend him.[72]

Paris steps forward and tells Romeo to stop what he is doing. Romeo, who fails to recognize Paris, tells him not to interfere. Paris insists and the two men begin to fight. Paris's page peers into the tomb to see what the commotion is, sees the two men fighting, and runs to call the watch. Romeo stabs Paris, who falls to the ground. With his dying breath, Paris asks Romeo to lay his body in the same tomb with Juliet. Romeo looks closer and realizes that the man he has just killed was Mercutio's cousin. He curses his luck and wonders if he is dreaming or if he is mad. He places Paris in the tomb with Juliet.

Romeo laments the death of his wife and comments on how beautiful she is even in death:

O my love, my wife,

Death, that hath suck'd the honey of thy breath,

Hath had no power yet upon thy beauty:

Thou art not conquer'd, beauty's ensign yet

Is crimson in thy lips and in thy cheeks,

And death's pale flag is not advanced there.[73]

Romeo then turns to Tybalt's body and asks for forgiveness. He then turns back to Juliet and promises that he will never leave her side. He drinks the poison that he bought from the apothecary, kisses Juliet, and dies.

After Romeo dies, Friar Lawrence enters the crypt with Balthasar. The two men discover that both Romeo and Paris are dead. While they are trying to make sense of the gruesome scene,

Juliet awakens from her sleep and is devastated to discover that Romeo has fatally poisoned himself.

Juliet awakens and sits upright in the tomb. Friar Lawrence is unhinged by this time, and hearing a noise outside the crypt he runs away without Juliet. Juliet comes to her senses, discovers the bodies of both Paris and Romeo, and is overcome by grief. She kisses Romeo and then stabs herself with his dagger.

Finally, the watchmen arrive at the crypt and one of them brings the frightened Friar Lawrence. Soon after the watchmen arrive, the Prince, the Montagues, and the Capulets arrive. The Prince demands to know what has happened, and Friar Lawrence tells him about Romeo and Juliet's secret courtship and marriage. He then tells the Prince about how Juliet was distressed because Romeo was banished for the death of Tybalt and she had been forced into a second marriage with Paris. Friar Lawrence also recounts his role in the scheme to fake Juliet's death and how his letter failed to reach Romeo in Mantua. At first the Prince does not believe the story, but when it is corroborated by Paris's page, Juliet's Nurse, and Balthasar, the Prince is forced to believe. Montague and Capulet, grief-stricken at their own roles in the tragedy, pledge to end their feud and build a monument to their children. The play ends with the Prince observing,

A glooming peace this morning with it brings,

The sun, for sorrow, will not show his head.

Go hence to have more talk of these sad things;

Some shall be pardon'd, and some punished:

For never was a story of more woe

Than this of Juliet and her Romeo.[74]

CHAPTER FOUR

The Characters of *Romeo and Juliet*

S hakespeare's plays are known for their rich characters, and it is easy to overlook the subtle impact that minor characters may have on the outcome of the plot. Likewise, it can sometimes be difficult to decipher the relationships between major characters. This type of complexity is pervasive in *Romeo and Juliet* because there are four major groups of characters interacting throughout the play: the Capulets, the Franciscans, the Montagues, and the Prince's Men.

Benvolio

Benvolio is a minor character who contributes to the plot in major ways. He is the nephew of Montague (Romeo's father), and Romeo's cousin. Benvolio, concerned about Romeo's love life, convinces Romeo to attend the Capulets' party. After Romeo kills Tybalt, it is Benvolio who encourages Romeo to flee, and it is Benvolio who explains to the Prince, the Capulets, and the Montagues how Romeo killed Tybalt.

Benvolio is a true friend: He is concerned about Romeo's well-being, stands by Romeo through thick and thin, and tries to defend Romeo's murder of Tybalt.

Capulet

Capulet refers to both the patriarch of the Capulet family (Juliet's father) and the surname of the family. Capulet is the head of a family that earned its wealth through trade, and he would like to see his daughter, Juliet, marry a man with a noble lineage, specifically Paris. At first, Capulet, like any doting father, advises Paris to "woo her . . . get her heart, / My will to her consent is but part; / And she agreed, within her scope of choice / Lies my consent and fair according voice."[75] However, later in the play Capulet shows his temper when Juliet refuses to marry Paris:

> Hang thee, young baggage! Disobedient wretch!
>
> I tell thee what: get thee to church a' Thursday,
>
> Or never after look me in the face.
>
> Speak not, reply not, do not answer me!
>
> My fingers itch. Wife, we scarce thought us blest
>
> That God had lent us but this only child,
>
> But now I see this one is one too much,
>
> And that we have a curse in having her.[76]

Capulet's sudden temper is evident in the first scene of the play when a brawl erupts and Capulet, despite his age, demands a weapon. Capulet is a character that can be very reasonable one moment, then become violent the next. He is also a character that is somewhat heavy-handed with his family, as evidenced by his treatment not only of Juliet but of Tybalt as well.

Escalus, the Prince of Verona

The Prince of Verona, Escalus, is another minor character who has a major impact on the play. The Prince acts as the voice of civil authority in *Romeo and Juliet* and condemns the feud between the Capulets and the Montagues as "brawls" that "Have thrice disturb'd the quiet of our streets."[77] He promises to punish both factions if the feuding continues. After the death of his kinsman, Mercutio, and Capulet's nephew, Tybalt, the Prince banishes Romeo and fines both the Capulets and the Montagues. The Prince's action leaves the way open for the mistakes and misunderstandings that lead to Romeo and Juliet's deaths.

Friar John

Friar John, although he appears in only one scene, has the greatest impact on the play of all the minor characters. Friar Lawrence gives a letter to Friar John to deliver to Romeo in Mantua. However, Friar John fails to give Romeo the letter because he visits a sick friend in Verona and is quarantined for fear of spreading the infection. Friar John's failure catapults *Romeo and Juliet* toward its tragic end.

Friar Lawrence

Romeo and Juliet is a play that is filled with minor characters that help move the action toward its final tragic conclusion. Friar Lawrence is instrumental in the play and acts as Romeo's confidant. He agrees to secretly marry Romeo and Juliet in the hope that the marriage will help "To turn your households' rancor to pure love."[78] Friar Lawrence also gives Juliet the sleeping potion that she drinks to avoid the marriage to Paris, and he gives a letter explaining the plan to Friar John to deliver to Romeo. However, Romeo never receives the letter and mistakenly believes that Juliet has actually died.

Juliet

Critics have often argued about the character of Juliet. Some critics have seen Juliet as "practical, incapable of romantic rhetoric . . . incapable of acting out the stereotypical role of the adolescent female languishing for a lover,"[79] while other critics have described her as an "inexperienced girl . . . trying to be more 'grown-up' than she really is."[80] Depending on the critic, Juliet is either a young woman who is wise beyond her years or a naive young girl suffering through her first "crush." Whatever the nature of Juliet's character, she is a key character in the play. Juliet is the only surviving child of Capulet and Lady Capulet and they want her to marry Paris. However, Juliet falls in love with Romeo and secretly marries the only son of her family's enemy, the Montagues. The secret love affair drives the play toward its tragic climax, which results in the deaths of both lovers.

Lady Capulet

Lady Capulet, Juliet's mother, seems to share her husband's ambitions to a certain extent. She also wants Juliet to marry Paris and advises her daughter to do so, saying Paris "Shall happily make thee . . . a joyful bride."[81] She also seems to share her husband's temper because after she learns of Tybalt's death, she pleads with the Prince for Romeo's death and lies in an attempt to get it. Regardless of Lady Capulet's shortcomings, she seems to honestly care for her daughter's welfare. When Capulet is berating Juliet for her refusal to marry Paris, Lady Capulet tries to calm him down. When Lady Capulet believes that Juliet is dead, her anguish is real:

Accurs'd, unhappy, wretched, hateful day!

Most miserable hour that e'er time saw

In lasting labor of his pilgrimage!

But one, poor one, one poor and loving child,

But one thing to rejoice and solace in,

And cruel Death hath catch'd it from my sight![82]

Mercutio

John Dryden wrote that "Shakespear show'd the best of his skill in his Mercutio, and he said himself, that he was forc'd to kill him in the third Act, to prevent being kill'd by him."[83] Mercutio is a kinsman to the Prince and one of the most enigmatic characters in the play. In the same way that the Nurse acts as a dramatic foil for Juliet, Mercutio's lustiness balances Romeo's romantic ideas of love. Mercutio mocks Romeo's

Actor John Barrymore (right) plays Mercutio in a 1936 film version of Romeo and Juliet.

love for Rosaline and later derides Romeo's notions of love and advises him, "If love be rough with you, be rough with love; / Prick love for pricking, and you beat love down."[84] However, Mercutio also has a loyal side, and he springs to Romeo's aid when he perceives that Romeo will not defend himself. Mercutio dies as a result of this intervention and curses both the Montagues and the Capulets: "A plague a' both your houses! / They have made worms' meat of me."[85] His curse is realized by the end of the play.

The Montagues

In contrast to the Capulets, the Montagues are not as fully developed characters. Montague, Romeo's father, appears in the play only three times. Lady Montague, Romeo's mother, speaks in the play only once. Despite this lack of development, it becomes obvious that the Montagues love their son as much as the Capulets love Juliet. In the first scene of the play, the Montagues are asking Benvolio to find out what is wrong with their son because "Could we but learn from whence his sorrow grow, / We would as willingly give cure as know."[86] Later in the play, after Romeo has killed Tybalt, Romeo's father defends his son's actions to the Prince, saying that Romeo was in the right because he had avenged Mercutio's death at Tybalt's hands. Finally, in the last scene of the play, Montague tells the Prince, "Alas, my liege, my wife is dead to-night; / Grief of my son's exile hath stopp'd her breath."[87] Even though the Montagues are not as fully developed as the Capulets and contribute little to the development of the play, they are important because they give the audience a sense of Romeo's background and help establish the idea that Romeo's parents love him as much as Juliet's parents love her.

The Nurse

Romeo and Juliet could not carry on their love affair without the help of Juliet's nurse. She is the character that acts as an intermediary between the two lovers and helps to arrange the secret marriage and the consummation of the marriage. The Nurse can be seen as the antithesis of Juliet: Juliet's sexual inexperience is offset by the Nurse's lustiness. Juliet's fidelity to Romeo is counterbalanced by the Nurse's fickleness. Juliet's naivete is neutralized by the Nurse's worldly wisdom. Aside from her roles as the facilitator of the forbidden romance and a foil for Juliet, the Nurse is also a source of comic relief. She tells bawdy stories, trades barbs with Mercutio, and slips a bit of sexual innuendo into the conversation whenever possible. In short, the Nurse's earthiness complements the divine love of Romeo and Juliet.

Paris

Like Mercutio, Paris is a kinsman to the Prince of Verona, and he is in love with Juliet. Initially, Paris is told by Capulet that if he can win Juliet's heart then Capulet will agree to the marriage. After the death of Tybalt, Capulet decides that Juliet should marry Paris whether he has her affection or not. Paris's love for Juliet is genuine, as shown by his outburst when told of her supposed death: "Beguil'd, divorced, wronged, spited, slain! / Most detestable Death, by thee beguil'd, / By cruel cruel thee quite overthrown! / O love, O life! Not life, but love in death!"[88] Paris later sneaks into Juliet's tomb to weep over her body and is surprised by Romeo. The two men fight and Romeo kills Paris, adding to the list of people killed by the feud between the Capulets and the Montagues.

Romeo

Of all the characters that Shakespeare created, Romeo is the most well known and the most beloved. Romeo is the only son of the Montagues, and he embodies all the qualities of the Renaissance idea of the courtly lover. In fact, critic H. A. Mason has described Romeo as "all sentiment,"[89] and Samuel Coleridge has described him as a young man in love with the idea of love: "Romeo became enamored of the idea he had formed in his own mind, and then . . . christened the first real being of the contrary sex as endowed with the perfections he desired. He appears to be in love with Rosaline; but, in truth, he is in love only with his own idea."[90] Indeed, when Romeo first enters the play he is lamenting the way his declared love, Rosaline, has been treating him, but the affection must not be too deep because the first time he sees Juliet he falls instantly and irrevocably in love: "Did my heart love till now? Forswear it, sight! / For I ne'er saw true beauty till this night."[91] Romeo's passion affects the play in other ways as well: It is his passion, and his failure to control it, that causes him to kill Tybalt and that forces him into exile. Despite Romeo's fickleness and immaturity, or maybe because of it, he is considered to be one of Shakespeare's most sympathetic characters.

Tybalt

Tybalt is the son of Lady Capulet's brother and is by extension Capulet's nephew and Juliet's cousin. Tybalt's name is borrowed from the medieval story of *Reynard the Fox*, which contains a character named "Tibalt" who is the Prince of the Cats. This provides the other characters in the play with material for punning on his name. Tybalt is the play's "hothead," a master swordsman who is ready to fight at the least provocation. He makes his feelings about the Montagues and peace clear in the first scene of the play: "What, drawn and talk of peace? I hate the word / As I hate hell, all Montagues, and thee."[92] Tybalt also does not forget a grudge. When Tybalt spies Romeo at the Capulets' party he wants to attack him, but he is restrained by Capulet. Feeling that his reputation has been tarnished, he vows revenge against Romeo. Tybalt's "hothead" and his thirst for revenge force Romeo to kill Tybalt despite the knowledge that doing so will ruin any chance that he and Juliet may have for a happy life.

CHAPTER FIVE

A Literary Analysis of *Romeo and Juliet*

Although most readers and viewers agree that *Romeo and Juliet* is an entertaining play, there is no consensus on the meaning of the play. Did Shakespeare intend the play as a celebration of young love or a condemnation of it? Or was he trying to dramatize youth in rebellion against old age? Is *Romeo and Juliet* truly a tragedy? Why are there so many paired opposites (love/hate, life/death) in the play? What roles do the sun, stars, moon, and heavens play? These questions remain the subject of conjecture and help explain why the play is still of interest to modern readers.

Love Conquers All?

The popular interpretation of *Romeo and Juliet* is that it is a play that celebrates love. The drama critic William Hazlitt wrote,

> *Romeo and Juliet* is the only tragedy which Shakespear has written entirely on a love story. . . . Romeo and Juliet are in love, but they are not love-sick. . . . Romeo is Hamlet

in love. There is the same rich exuberance of passion and sentiment in the one, that there is of thought and sentiment in the other. Both are absent and self-involved, both live out of themselves in a world of imagination . . . Romeo is abstracted from everything but his love.[93]

The character of Romeo is supposed to represent the typical courtly lover. *Benet's Reader's Encyclopedia* defines "courtly love" as

A medieval code of attitudes toward love and of the tightly conventionalized conduct considered suitable for noble lords and ladies. It postulates the adoration and respect of a gallant and courageous knight or courtier for a beautiful, intelligent, lofty-minded noblewoman, who usually remains chaste and unattainable. . . . Nevertheless, the lover welcomes the suffering of his passion, for it ennobles him and inspires him to great achievements.[94]

When Romeo first appears on the stage, he is lamenting the fact that the object of his affection, Rosaline, does not share his love. He voices his frustration by using language reminiscent of courtly lovers, such as "Out of her favor where I am in love," "she'll not be hit / with Cupid's arrow," and "She hath forsworn to love, and in that vow / Do I live dead that live to tell it now."[95] This has the effect of making Romeo seem like a lovesick boy, or as Samuel Coleridge said, "He appears to be in love with Rosaline; but, in truth, he is in love with only his idea."[96]

However, when Romeo first sees Juliet and falls truly in love, the language that he uses to express his love is fresh and fails to use the language of courtly love: "O, she doth teach the torches to burn bright! / It seems she hangs upon the cheek of night / As rich a jewel in an Ethiop's ear— / Beauty too rich for use, for earth too dear!"[97] Romeo does not speak of Juliet as unattainable and cruel but as attainable and kind. The change of language is meant to represent how true love has transformed Romeo from a lovesick boy into a man in love.

Likewise, love recasts Juliet from the demure girl who is eager to please her father to a young woman who disobeys her parents out of love. In the balcony scene, Juliet asks Romeo point-blank, "Dost thou love me?"[98] But as Romeo begins to swear his love, Juliet stops him and tells him the only oath she will accept is the oath of marriage, even though she knows her father wants her to marry Paris. One critic has described Juliet as "practical, incapable of romantic rhetoric"[99] and this can be seen in the simple way that Juliet tells Romeo about her feelings.

Aside from love changing both Romeo and Juliet, love also acts as "the teacher of society."[100] The prologue makes it clear that the love of Romeo and Juliet will "bury their parents' strife"[101] but only with their deaths. The idea of sacrificing innocent children for the punishment of sinful parents is an ancient belief that can be traced back to the Bible, and in *Romeo and Juliet* it is given a new twist: The fatal love of their children causes the warring families to learn to love each other. In *Romeo and Juliet*, Shakespeare celebrates the healing power of love and shows, how even in death, love conquers all. At least one critic has observed that "the lovers are allowed only the choice of death,"[102] because it is only through their deaths that the feud can be put to rest.

Some scholars have seen *Romeo and Juliet* not as a celebration of young love but a criticism of it. They base this assertion on the fact that when Shakespeare married Anne Hathaway she was already three months' pregnant and was eight years older than her husband. They assume that Shakespeare regretted this decision and point to the role that "haste" plays in *Romeo and Juliet*. Romeo meets and marries Juliet, kills Tybalt, flees to Mantua, returns to Verona, kills Paris, kills himself, and Juliet commits suicide within the scope of three days. Friar Lawrence warns Romeo against haste, "Wisely and slow, they stumble that run fast," and to "love moderately: long love doth so / Too swift arrives as tardy as too slow,"[103] but Romeo and Juliet are always in a hurry. Scholars who favor this interpretation say that this emphasis on haste implies Shakespeare's dissatisfaction with his own hurried marriage and acts as a warning against the foolhardiness of young love. However, as S. Schoenbaum, one of Shakespeare's biographers, has observed, "We do well to remind ourselves that these comments are spoken not by the author in his own voice, but by the shadows he created."[104]

Sources of Conflict

Romeo and Juliet is a play about conflict. The prologue informs the audience that Verona is a city in conflict: "Two households, both alike in dignity, / In fair Verona, where we lay our scene, / From ancient grudge break to new mutiny, / Where civil blood makes civil hands unclean."[105] The first scene also illustrates this conflict by the argument between servants of the Capulets and Montagues that escalates to a street brawl between Tybalt and Benvolio and eventually draws in old Capulet and old Montague. There are at least two sources for this conflict in *Romeo and Juliet.*

One source of the conflict is the "generation gap" between the adults in the play and the youths. This generation gap is apparent in the first scene of the play when the fighting is done by the servants and young people, while old Montague and old Capulet are prevented from joining the fight because of their infirmities. Even though it is "their parents' strife,"[106] their children and servants must fight the feud for them because they are unable. Indeed, Northrop Frye has observed that Romeo, Juliet, Benvolio, and Mercutio "seem to care very little about the feud"[107] and are only drawn into the feud because of their parents or friends. In a sense, it is Romeo and Juliet's attempt to rise above the feud that dooms them.

Coppelia Kahn has observed, "*Romeo and Juliet* is about a pair of adolescents trying to grow up. Growing up requires that

they separate themselves from their parents by forming an intimate bond with one of the opposite sex which supercedes filial
bonds."[108] Because Romeo and Juliet are forced to keep their
bond a secret, it causes the play to become a tragedy of misunderstandings and accidents. If the marriage had been public,
Mercutio would not have been killed by Tybalt, and Romeo
would not in turn be forced to kill Tybalt in vengeance. Likewise,
Juliet would not have to drink the sleeping potion to avoid the
marriage to Paris. It has been argued that "the feud . . . is the primary tragic force in the play . . . [and] Shakespeare shows [it] to
be tragically self-destructive."[109]

Another source of conflict in the play arises from the effect
that the private grudge between the two families has on the
public order of Verona. This effect can be seen in the opening
scene of the play when the brawl between the Capulets and
the Montagues causes the citizens of Verona to take to the
streets calling for the downfall of both families: "Down with
the Capulets! Down with the Montagues!"[110] The Prince
emphasizes the effect the feud has had on the public order of
Verona when he proclaims,

Three civil brawls, bred of an airy word,

By thee, old Capulet, and Montague,

Have thrice disturb'd the quiet of our streets,

And made Verona's ancient citizens

Cast by their grave beseeming ornaments

To wield old partisans, in hands as old,

Cank'red with peace, to part your cank'red hate;

If ever you disturb our streets again

Your lives shall pay the forfeit of the peace.[111]

Both the Prince and the citizens are tired of the feud and long for peace; however, the old hatreds die hard. Frank Kermode has observed that "the hot blood which makes love at once a matter of rapture and low jokes is the same that keeps warm the obsolete Montague-Capulet feud."[112]

It is the threat of the feud that is always boiling beneath the surface in *Romeo and Juliet*. Old Capulet must threaten Tybalt to keep him from attacking Romeo at the party; Juliet worries that Romeo will be discovered in the garden and killed; and Friar Lawrence hopes that, by marrying Romeo and Juliet, "this alliance may so happy prove / To turn your households' rancor to pure love."[113] Despite the hopes of Friar Lawrence, the marriage does not ease the tensions between the two families but once again causes a public street brawl, one that results in the deaths of Mercutio and Tybalt. This causes the Prince to comment, "My blood for your rude brawls doth lie a-bleeding."[114] The private grudge between the Capulets and the Montagues not only results in the disruption of public order but also causes the deaths of innocent people such as Mercutio and, later, Paris. Shakespeare seems to be illustrating the tragic nature of such feuds in *Romeo and Juliet* and how such grudges can only result in death and sadness for all the participants.

Opposites and Paradoxes

A casual reading of *Romeo and Juliet* reveals that the play is built around opposites. The themes of the play (love/hate, youth/age, life/death, private feud/public order) fight for supremacy throughout the play. By linking these ideas together, Shakespeare is making the play more dramatic and underscoring the strengths and weaknesses of each idea. For instance, by setting the love story of Romeo and Juliet against a backdrop of familial hate, he demonstrates the fragile nature of love and the consuming nature of hatred.

In the same way, the characters of the play also have opposites. The courtly love of Romeo is balanced by the earthly love

of Mercutio, the sexual innocence and loyalty of Juliet are counterbalanced by the Nurse's carnal knowledge and shifting loyal-
ties, the peace-loving Benvolio is offset by the warmongering
Tybalt, and the irrational hatred of Capulet and Montague is
counteracted by the rational Prince and Friar Lawrence. By pair-
ing the characters in this way, Shakespeare is better able to illus-
trate the themes of the play in a subtle manner.

This exploration of paradoxes can also be found in the language of the play itself. Romeo speaks of "brawling love" and
"loving hate,"[115] he describes love as "A choking gall, and a
preserving sweet,"[116] and he describes Juliet as "a snowy dove
trooping with crows."[117] Juliet says, "My only love sprung
from my only hate,"[118] and proclaims that "My grave is like to
be my wedding-bed."[119] The effect of this paradoxical language makes the dramatic action of the play more intense. In
Romeo and Juliet, there are no neutral areas because every
character is either on one side or the other.

Dreams

Dreams also play a large role in *Romeo and Juliet*. Before
Benvolio, Mercutio, and Romeo attend the Capulets' feast,
Romeo expresses his misgivings about attending the feast
because of a dream. This causes Mercutio to declare that
"dreamers often lie,"[120] and he proceeds to give the Queen
Mab soliloquy, which he concludes by describing dreams as
"the children of an idle brain."[121] The characters in *Romeo and
Juliet* can be divided into two categories: those, like Mercutio,
who do not believe in dreams and those, like Romeo, who do.

Dreams are used throughout the play for foreshadowing.
However, at a critical moment in the play, Mercutio's comment that "dreamers often lie" is proven true. When Romeo
is in Mantua, he has a dream that gives him hope:

If I may trust the flattering truth of sleep,

My dreams presage some joyful news at hand. . . .

I dreamt my lady came and found me dead—

Strange dream, that gives a dead man leave to think!

And breath'd such life with kisses in my lips

that I reviv'd.[122]

But Romeo's dream is not to be. When Juliet awakens in the crypt and finds Romeo dead, she kisses him in an attempt to die herself, not to breathe life back into him. The role that dreams play in *Romeo and Juliet* is twofold: They act as harbingers of what is to come and what is not to be.

What Role Does Fate Play?

Critics have often argued about the role of fate in *Romeo and Juliet*. The stars, for instance, are used by Shakespeare to symbolize the unavoidable. From the very beginning of the play, the audience knows that the tragic future of the "star-cross'd lovers"[123] is sealed. Elizabethans generally accepted the belief "that the stars dictated the general mutability of sublunary things, and that fortune was a part of this mutability applying to mankind alone."[124] This idea is so strong that audiences still recognize the reference to astrology today. Even though Elizabethans believed that the stars influenced earthly events, they also believed that "man has it in him to survive the blows of fortune."[125]

Critics have denounced *Romeo and Juliet* as a tragedy because the characters lack the traditional "tragic flaw" that propels other tragic heroes to their ultimate fates. Instead, the play relies on chance (Romeo meeting Juliet at the Capulets' party, Romeo meeting Tybalt on the street after his marriage, Friar Lawrence's undelivered letter, Romeo and Paris meeting in the Capulet tomb) to move the play to its tragic conclusion. These critics reason that, since the lovers' demise is due to "fate" and not to any character flaw, the play is not a tragedy in the truest sense of the word. However, other critics claim

Some critics believe that the tragic flaw of Romeo and Juliet *can be found in the couple's love for each other, which is too perfect and passionate for the world around them.*

that the tragic flaw can be found in Romeo and Juliet's love: It is too perfect and too passionate for their world. They argue that the Verona in which Romeo and Juliet exist is not ready for such love and that only through their deaths can the city heal itself of the hate that is tearing it apart.

Notes

Chapter 1: The Life of William Shakespeare

1. William Shakespeare, *The Tragedy of Richard III*, in *The Riverside Shakespeare*, ed. G. Blakemore Evans. Boston: Houghton Mifflin, 1974, p. 713 (I.i.54–55).

2. William Shakespeare, *The Tragedy of Romeo and Juliet*, in *The Riverside Shakespeare*, p. 1,069 (II.ii.156–57).

3. William Shakespeare, *The Taming of the Shrew*, in *The Riverside Shakespeare*, p. 127 (III.ii.150).

4. Ben Jonson, "To the Memory of My Beloved, the Author, Mr. William Shakespeare, and What He Hath Left Us," in M. H. Abrams, ed., *The Norton Anthology of English Literature*, vol. 1, 6th ed., New York: W. W. Norton, 1993, p. 1,242.

5. Edmund Chambers, *A Short Life of Shakespeare with the Sources*, ed. Charles Williams. London: Oxford University Press, 1963, p. 14.

6. Quoted in S. Schoenbaum, *William Shakespeare: A Compact Documentary Life*. New York: Oxford University Press, 1987, p. 73.

7. William Shakespeare, *A Midsummer Night's Dream*, in *The Riverside Shakespeare*, p. 230 (II.ii.41–42, 56–59).

8. Shakespeare, *The Tragedy of Romeo and Juliet*, p. 1,069 (II.ii.109–11, 143–46).

9. Shakespeare, *The Taming of the Shrew*, p. 117 (I.ii.50–52).

10. Quoted in Levi Fox, *The Shakespeare Handbook*. Boston: G. K. Hall, 1987, p. 92.

11. Robert Greene, "Life Records and Contemporary References," in *The Riverside Shakespeare*, p. 1,835.

12. Greene, "Life Records and Contemporary References," p. 1,835.

13. Quoted in Schoenbaum, *William Shakespeare*, p. 176.

14. Shakespeare, "Venus and Adonis," in *The Riverside Shakespeare*, p. 1,705.

15. Nicholas Rowe, *Some Account of the Life &c. of Mr. William Shakespear*, at *The Shakespeare Resource Page*, http://daphne. palomar.edu/SHAKESPEARE/rowe.htm.

16. Quoted in Schoenbaum, *William Shakespeare*, p. 249.

17. Quoted in James Joyce, *Ulysses.* New York: Randon Books, 1914.

Chapter 2: The History of *Romeo and Juliet*

18. Frank Kermode, introduction to *The Tragedy of Romeo and Juliet*, in *The Riverside Shakespeare*, pp. 1,055–56.

19. Francis Meres, "Early Critical Comment on the Plays and Poems," in *The Riverside Shakespeare*, p. 1,844.

20. Ben Jonson, "Early Critical Comment on the Plays and Poems," in *The Riverside Shakespeare*, p. 1,847.

21. John Dryden, "Early Critical Comment on the Plays and Poems," in *The Riverside Shakespeare*, p. 1,848.

22. Kermode, introduction to *The Tragedy of Romeo and Juliet*, in *The Riverside Shakespeare*, p. 1,055.

23. Quoted in Frank Kermode, introduction to *The Tragedy of Titus Andronicus*, in *The Riverside Shakespeare*, p. 1,019.

24. Samuel Pepys, "Romeo and Juliet," in F. E. Halliday, ed., *Shakespeare and His Critics.* New York: Schocken Books, 1963, p. 157.

Chapter 3: The Plot of *Romeo and Juliet*

25. Shakespeare, *The Tragedy of Romeo and Juliet*, p. 1,059 (I.i.66–67).

26. Shakespeare, *The Tragedy of Romeo and Juliet*, p. 1,059 (I.i.74).

27. Shakespeare, *The Tragedy of Romeo and Juliet*, p. 1,060 (I.i.163).

28. Shakespeare, *The Tragedy of Romeo and Juliet*, p. 1,061 (I.i.190–94).

29. Shakespeare, *The Tragedy of Romeo and Juliet*, p. 1,061 (I.i.228).

30. Shakespeare, *The Tragedy of Romeo and Juliet*, p. 1,061 (I.ii.8–11).

31. Shakespeare, *The Tragedy of Romeo and Juliet*, p. 1,062 (I.ii.87).

32. Shakespeare, *The Tragedy of Romeo and Juliet*, p. 1,063 (I.iii.97–99).

33. Shakespeare, *The Tragedy of Romeo and Juliet*, p. 1,064 (I.iv.52).

34. Shakespeare, *The Tragedy of Romeo and Juliet*, p. 1,064 (I.iv.54, 59, 67).

35. Shakespeare, *The Tragedy of Romeo and Juliet*, p. 1,065 (I.iv.97).

36. Shakespeare, *The Tragedy of Romeo and Juliet*, p. 1,065 (I.iv.106–109).

37. Shakespeare, *The Tragedy of Romeo and Juliet*, p. 1,066 (I.v.52–53).

38. Shakespeare, *The Tragedy of Romeo and Juliet*, p. 1,066 (I.v.61–63).

39. Shakespeare, *The Tragedy of Romeo and Juliet*, p. 1,066 (I.v.91–92).

40. Shakespeare, *The Tragedy of Romeo and Juliet*, p. 1,066 (I.v.97).

41. Shakespeare, *The Tragedy of Romeo and Juliet*, p. 1,067 (I.v.138–41).

42 Shakespeare, *The Tragedy of Romeo and Juliet*, p. 1,067 (II.Chorus.13–14).

43 Shakespeare, *The Tragedy of Romeo and Juliet*, p. 1,068 (II.ii.33–36).

44. Shakespeare, *The Tragedy of Romeo and Juliet*, p. 1,069 (II.ii.109–11).

45. Shakespeare, *The Tragedy of Romeo and Juliet*, p. 1,069 (II.ii.116–20).

46. Shakespeare, *The Tragedy of Romeo and Juliet*, p. 1,069 (II.ii.143–48).

47. Shakespeare, *The Tragedy of Romeo and Juliet*, p. 1,070 (II.ii.184–85).

48. Shakespeare, *The Tragedy of Romeo and Juliet*, p. 1,070 (II.iii.22–23).

49. Shakespeare, *The Tragedy of Romeo and Juliet*, p. 1,070 (II.iii.49, 57–58).

50. Shakespeare, *The Tragedy of Romeo and Juliet*, p. 1,074 (II.vi.11–15).

51. Shakespeare, *The Tragedy of Romeo and Juliet*, p. 1,074 (III.i.1–4).

52. Shakespeare, *The Tragedy of Romeo and Juliet*, p. 1,075 (III.i.68–72).

53. Shakespeare, *The Tragedy of Romeo and Juliet*, p. 1,076 (III.i.106–107).

54. Shakespeare, *The Tragedy of Romeo and Juliet*, p. 1,076 (III.i.125–29).

55. Shakespeare, *The Tragedy of Romeo and Juliet*, p. 1,076 (III.i.136).

56. Shakespeare, *The Tragedy of Romeo and Juliet*, p. 1,078 (III.ii.90–92).

57. Shakespeare, *The Tragedy of Romeo and Juliet*, p. 1,078 (III.ii.137).

58. Shakespeare, *The Tragedy of Romeo and Juliet*, p. 1,079 (III.iii.29–33).

59. Shakespeare, *The Tragedy of Romeo and Juliet*, pp. 1,079–80 (III.iii.108–14).

60. Shakespeare, *The Tragedy of Romeo and Juliet*, p. 1,081 (III.v.52–53).

61. Shakespeare, *The Tragedy of Romeo and Juliet*, p. 1,081 (III.v.55–56).

62. Shakespeare, *The Tragedy of Romeo and Juliet*, p. 1,082 (III.v.156, 160).

63. Shakespeare, *The Tragedy of Romeo and Juliet*, p. 1,082 (III.v.164–67).

64. Shakespeare, *The Tragedy of Romeo and Juliet*, p. 1,083 (III.v.192).

65. Shakespeare, *The Tragedy of Romeo and Juliet*, p. 1,084 (IV.i.18).

66. Shakespeare, *The Tragedy of Romeo and Juliet*, p. 1,084 (IV.i.106).

67. Shakespeare, *The Tragedy of Romeo and Juliet*, p. 1,085 (IV.ii.22).

68. Shakespeare, *The Tragedy of Romeo and Juliet*, p. 1,087 (IV.v.25–27).

69. Shakespeare, *The Tragedy of Romeo and Juliet*, p. 1,088 (V.i.2).

70. Shakespeare, *The Tragedy of Romeo and Juliet*, p. 1,088 (V.i.27–29).

71. Shakespeare, *The Tragedy of Romeo and Juliet*, p. 1,088 (V.i.34).

72. Shakespeare, *The Tragedy of Romeo and Juliet*, p. 1,090 (V.iii.49–53).

73. Shakespeare, *The Tragedy of Romeo and Juliet*, p. 1,090 (V.iii.91–96).

74. Shakespeare, *The Tragedy of Romeo and Juliet*, p. 1,093 (V.iii.305–10).

Chapter 4: The Characters of *Romeo and Juliet*

75. Shakespeare, *The Tragedy of Romeo and Juliet*, p. 1,061 (I.ii.16–19).

76. Shakespeare, *The Tragedy of Romeo and Juliet*, p. 1,082 (III.v.160–67).

77. Shakespeare, *The Tragedy of Romeo and Juliet*, p. 1,059 (I.i.89–91).

78. Shakespeare, *The Tragedy of Romeo and Juliet*, p. 1,071 (II.iii.92).

79. Evelyn Gajowski, *The Art of Loving: Female Subjectivity and Male Discursive Traditions in Shakespeare's Tragedies.* Newark: University of Delaware Press, 1992, pp. 33–35.

80. Clifford Leech, "The Moral Tragedy of *Romeo and Juliet*," in Joseph A. Porter, ed., *Critical Essays on Shakespeare's* Romeo and Juliet. New York: G. K. Hall, 1997, p. 13.

81. Shakespeare, *The Tragedy of Romeo and Juliet*, p. 1,082 (III.v.115).

82. Shakespeare, *The Tragedy of Romeo and Juliet*, p. 1,087 (IV.v.43–48).

83. John Dryden, "Romeo and Juliet," in Halliday, *Shakespeare and His Critics*, p. 158.

84. Shakespeare, *The Tragedy of Romeo and Juliet*, p. 1,064 (I.iv.27–28).

85. Shakespeare, *The Tragedy of Romeo and Juliet*, p. 1,076 (III.i.106–107).

86. Shakespeare, *The Tragedy of Romeo and Juliet*, p. 1,060 (I.i.154–55).

87. Shakespeare, *The Tragedy of Romeo and Juliet*, p. 1,092 (V.iii.210–11).

88. Shakespeare, *The Tragedy of Romeo and Juliet*, p. 1,087 (IV.v.55–58).

89. H. A. Mason, *Shakespeare's Tragedies of Love*. London: Chatto and Windus, 1970, p. 48.

90. Samuel Coleridge, "Romeo and Juliet," in Halliday, *Shakespeare and His Critics*, p. 160.

91. Shakespeare, *The Tragedy of Romeo and Juliet*, p. 1,066 (I.v.52–53).

92. Shakespeare, *The Tragedy of Romeo and Juliet*, p. 1,059 (I.i.70–71).

Chapter 5: A Literary Analysis of *Romeo and Juliet*

93. William Hazlitt, "Romeo and Juliet," in Halliday, *Shakespeare and His Critics*, pp. 158–59.

94. Katherine Baker Siepmann, ed., *Benet's Reader's Encyclopedia*, 3rd ed. New York: Harper and Row, 1987, pp. 218–19.

95. Shakespeare, *The Tragedy of Romeo and Juliet*, pp. 1,060–61 (I.i.168, 208–209, 223–224).

96. Coleridge, "Romeo and Juliet," p. 160.

97. Shakespeare, *The Tragedy of Romeo and Juliet*, p. 1,066 (I.v.44–47).

98. Shakespeare, *The Tragedy of Romeo and Juliet*, p. 1,068 (II.ii.90).

99. Gajowski, *The Art of Loving*, p. 35.

100. Donald A. Stauffer, "The School of Love: *Romeo and Juliet*," in Alfred Harbage, ed., *Shakespeare: The Tragedies*. Englewood Cliffs, NJ: Prentice Hall, 1964, p. 29.

101. Shakespeare, *The Tragedy of Romeo and Juliet*, p. 1,058 (prologue.8).

102. Mason, *Shakespeare's Tragedies of Love*, p. 50.

103. Shakespeare, *The Tragedy of Romeo and Juliet*, pp. 1,071 (II.iii.94), 1,074 (II.vi.14–15).

104. Schoenbaum, *William Shakespeare*, p. 83.

105. Shakespeare, *The Tragedy of Romeo and Juliet*, p. 1,058 (prologue.1–4).

106. Shakespeare, *The Tragedy of Romeo and Juliet*, p. 1,058 (prologue.8).

107. Northrop Frye, *Northrop Frye on Shakespeare*, ed. Robert Sandler. New Haven, CT: Yale University Press, 1986, p. 16.

108. Coppelia Kahn, "Coming of Age in Verona," in Mark Rose, ed., *Shakespeare's Early Tragedies: A Collection of Critical Essays*. Englewood Cliffs, NJ: Prentice Hall, 1995, p. 182.

109. Kahn, "Coming of Age in Verona," p. 182.

110. Shakespeare, *The Tragedy of Romeo and Juliet*, p. 1,059 (I.i.74).

111. Shakespeare, *The Tragedy of Romeo and Juliet*, pp. 1,059–60 (I.i.89–97).

112. Kermode, introduction to *The Tragedy of Romeo and Juliet*, p. 1,056.

113. Shakespeare, *The Tragedy of Romeo and Juliet*, p. 1,071 (II.iii.91–92).

114. Shakespeare, *The Tragedy of Romeo and Juliet*, p. 1,077 (III.i.189).

115. Shakespeare, *The Tragedy of Romeo and Juliet*, p. 1,060 (I.i.176).

116. Shakespeare, *The Tragedy of Romeo and Juliet*, p. 1,061 (I.i.193).

117. Shakespeare, *The Tragedy of Romeo and Juliet*, p. 1,066 (I.v.48).

118. Shakespeare, *The Tragedy of Romeo and Juliet*, p. 1,067 (I.v.138).

119. Shakespeare, *The Tragedy of Romeo and Juliet*, p. 1,067 (I.v.135).

120. Shakespeare, *The Tragedy of Romeo and Juliet*, p. 1,064 (I.iv.52).

121. Shakespeare, *The Tragedy of Romeo and Juliet*, p. 1,065 (I.iv.97).

122. Shakespeare, *The Tragedy of Romeo and Juliet*, p. 1,088 (V.i.1–9).

123. Shakespeare, *The Tragedy of Romeo and Juliet*, p. 1,058 (prologue.6).

124. E. M. W. Tillyard, *The Elizabethan World Picture*. New York: Vintage Books, ca. 1942, p. 53.

125. Tillyard, *The Elizabethan World Picture*, p. 56.

For Further Exploration

1. Reread Mercutio's "Queen Mab" soliloquy (act 1, scene 4, lines 53–94). Why do you think Shakespeare included this speech in *Romeo and Juliet?* What is the meaning of this speech? Would you say this is the best soliloquy in the play? Why or why not? *See also:* John Dryden, *In Praise of Mercutio;* Ben Jonson, *Ben Jonson Responds to John Dryden's Criticisms of Shakespeare;* Samuel Coleridge, *Coleridge on Mercutio.*

2. Reread the scenes in which Romeo and Juliet are together (act 1, scene 5; act 2, scene 2; act 2, scene 6; act 3, scene 5; and act 5, scene 3). Notice that all of the scenes, except one (act 2, scene 6), take place at night or in the hours just before dawn. What reason do you think Shakespeare had for doing this? Also notice that during the entire play, the lovers are together in only five scenes. Why do you think Shakespeare allowed them to be together in only five scenes? *See also:* Michael Goldman, *The Theatrical Experience of* Romeo and Juliet.

3. Think about how the characters are paired with opposites (Romeo/Mercutio, Juliet/the Nurse, Benvolio/Tybalt, Capulet-Montague/the Prince–Friar Lawrence). How are the characters similar? How are the characters different? Think about Romeo and Juliet. In what way are they the same? How are they different?

4. The story line of doomed lovers caught between warring factions was not a new idea when Shakespeare wrote *Romeo and Juliet.* Shakespeare's play, in fact, bears some resemblance to the mythological story of "Pyramus and Thisbe." Research the story of Pyramus and Thisbe at your local library (*Bullfinch's Mythology,* compiled by Bryan Holme, is an excellent source for the story) and compare it with Shakespeare's *Romeo and Juliet.* How are the two stories similar? How are the stories different? What do you think accounts for the difference?

5. In Shakespeare's time, plays that contained a marriage were thought of as "comedies." The first half of *Romeo and Juliet* is filled with many jokes, slapstick humor, and a marriage. What changes this potential "comedy" into a "tragedy"? Why? Do you think Shakespeare was violating dramatic standards of the time on purpose? What dramatic purpose does this change from comedy to tragedy serve in the play? *See also:* Susan Snyder, *Comedy and Tragedy;* H. B. Charlton, *Romeo and Juliet as a Dramatic Experiment.*

6. *Romeo and Juliet* was written more than four hundred years ago, yet it remains one of the most frequently produced plays. In fact,

Romeo and Juliet has been translated into the majority of the world's languages, and the play itself has been reinterpreted over the years. The story of Romeo and Juliet has been told as a ballet by Kenneth MacMillan, it has been the subject of an opera by Gounod, it has been the topic of Hollywood movies and foreign films, and it has even been retold as a Broadway musical (*West Side Story*). What do you think accounts for the popularity of *Romeo and Juliet*? View a film adaptation of *Romeo and Juliet*. How is the film similar to the play? How are they different?

7. Most children rebel against their parents during their teenage years. Do you think *Romeo and Juliet* is about two young people rebelling against their parents' wishes? Specifically, what in the play leads you to your conclusion? *See also:* Coppelia Kahn, *Romeo, Juliet, and the Capulet-Montague Feud.*

8. Reread the end of *Romeo and Juliet* (act 5, scene 3). The Prince proclaims that "Some shall be pardon'd, and some punished." Think about the role that each character played in the tragedy. Which characters should be pardoned and which characters should be punished? What in the play leads you to your judgments?

9. Reread the definition of "courtly love" in the literary analysis chapter of this book. Think about Romeo's attitude toward Rosaline (refer to act 1, scene 1, lines 159–238) and compare it with the way he treats Juliet. In what ways is Romeo like a courtly lover? In what ways is he different? Do you think Shakespeare was praising the idea of courtly love or criticizing it? What in the play leads you to your conclusion? *See also:* Northrop Frye, *The Role of Courtly Love in Romeo and Juliet;* Rosalie Colie, *The Influence of Sonnets.*

10. The character of Mercutio is a favorite of audiences but critics have argued about the dramatic purpose of the character. Some critics have hailed Mercutio as Shakespeare's finest character, while others have dismissed him as unnecessary to the action of the play. Which critic do you agree with? Why? What in *Romeo and Juliet* leads you to your conclusion about Mercutio? *See also:* John Dryden, *In Praise of Mercutio;* Ben Jonson, *Ben Johnson's Responds to John Dryden's Criticisms of Shakespeare;* Samuel Coleridge, *Coleridge on Mercutio.*

11. The character of Romeo has been criticized because he falls short of the tragic stature of Shakespeare's later heroes such as Othello, Hamlet, Macbeth, and King Lear. Is the character of Romeo a failure as a tragic hero? Why or why not? What in the play leads you to your conclusion? *See also:* William Hazlitt, *Romeo Is Hamlet in Love;* Evelyn Gajowski, *Romeo and Revenge.*

89

Appendix of Criticism

Contemporary Criticism

Early Praise for Shakespeare

As Plautus and Seneca are accounted the best for comedy and tragedy among the Latins: so Shakespeare among the English is the most excellent in both kinds for the stage; for Comedy, witness his [*Two*] *Gentlemen of Verona*, his [*Comedy of*] *Errors*, his *Love Labors Lost*, his *Love Labors Won* [this is thought to have been one of Shakespeare's "lost" plays], his *Midsummer's Night Dream*, & his *Merchant of Venice*: for Tragedy his *Richard the 2*, *Richard the 3*, *Henry the 4*, *King John*, *Titus Andronicus* and his *Romeo and Juliet*.

> Francis Meres, in *The Riverside Shakespeare*. Boston: Houghton Mifflin, 1974.

An Unhappy Theatergoer Comments on *Romeo and Juliet*

March 1, 1662: To the Opera, and there saw *Romeo and Juliet*, the first time it was ever acted, but it is a play of itself the worst that ever I heard, and the worst acted that ever I saw these people do, and I am resolved to go no more to see the first time of acting, for they were all of them out more or less.

> Samuel Pepys, in F. E. Halliday, ed., *Shakespeare and His Critics*. New York: Schocken Books, 1963.

John Dryden Criticizes Shakespeare's Difficult Language

Yet it must be allow'd to the present Age, that the tongue in general is so much refin'd since Shakespear's time, that many of his words, and more of his Phrases, are scarce intelligible. And of those which we understand some are ungrammatical, others course [coarse]; and his whole style is so pester'd with Figurative expressions, that it is as affected as it is obscure. . . . If Shakespear be allow'd, as I think he must, to have made his characters distinct, it will easily be infer'd that he understood the nature of the Passions: because it has been prov'd already, that confus'd passions make undistinguishable characters: yet I cannot deny that he has his failings: but they are not so much in the passions themselves, as in his manner of expression: he often obscures his meaning by his words, and sometimes makes it unintelligible.

90

John Dryden, in *The Riverside Shakespeare*. Boston:
Houghton Mifflin, 1974.

In Praise of Mercutio

Shakespear show'd the best of his skill in his Mercutio, and he said himself, that he was forc'd to kill him in the third Act, to prevent being kill'd by him. But, for my part, I cannot find he was so dangerous a person: I see nothing in him but what was so exceeding harmless, that he might have liv'd to the end of the Play, and dy'd in his bed, without offence to any man.

John Dryden, in F. E. Halliday, ed., *Shakespeare and His
Critics*. New York: Schocken Books, 1963.

Ben Jonson Responds to John Dryden's Criticisms of Shakespeare

This play [*Romeo and Juliet*] is one of the most pleasing of our author's [Shakespeare's] performances. The scenes are busy and various, the incidents numerous and important, the catastrophe irresistibly affecting, and the process of the action carried on with such probability, at least with such congruity to popular opinions, as tragedy requires.

Here is one of the few attempts of Shakespeare to exhibit the conversation of gentlemen, to represent the airy sprightliness of juvenile elegance. Mr. Dryden mentions a tradition . . . of a declaration made by Shakespeare, that 'he was obliged to kill Mercutio in the third act, lest he should have been killed by him.' Yet he thinks him 'no such formidable person, but that he might have lived through the play, and died in his bed,' without danger to the poet. . . . Mercutio's wit, gaiety and courage, will always procure him friends that wish him a longer life; but his death is not precipitated, he has lived out the time allotted him in the construction of the play; nor do I doubt the ability of Shakespeare to have continued his existence, though some of his sallies are, perhaps, out of reach of Dryden; whose genius was not very fertile of merriment, nor ductile to humour, but acute, argumentative, comprehensive, and sublime.

Ben Jonson, in F. E. Halliday, ed., *Shakespeare and His
Critics*. New York: Schocken Books, 1963.

Eighteenth- and Nineteenth-Century Criticism

Coleridge on Mercutio

Mercutio is a man possessing all the elements of a poet: the whole world was, as it were, subject to his law of association. . . . This faculty, moreover, is combined with the manners and feelings of a perfect gentleman, himself utterly unconscious of his powers. By his loss it was contrived that the whole catastrophe of the tragedy should be brought about: it endears him to Romeo, and gives to the death of Mercutio an importance which it could not otherwise have acquired.

I say this in answer to an observation, I think by Dryden (to which indeed Dr. Johnson has fully replied), that Shakespeare having carried the part of Mercutio as far as he could, till his genius was exhausted, had killed him in the third Act, to get him out of the way. What shallow nonsense! As I have remarked, upon the death of Mercutio the whole catastrophe depends; it is produced by it. . . . Had not Mercutio been rendered so amiable and so interesting, we could not have felt so strongly the necessity of Romeo's interference, connecting it immediately, and passionately, with the future fortunes of the lover and his mistress.

> Samuel Coleridge, in F. E. Halliday, ed., *Shakespeare and His Critics.* New York: Schocken Books, 1963.

Romeo Is Hamlet in Love

Romeo and Juliet is the only tragedy which Shakespear has written entirely on a love-story. It is supposed to have been his first play, and it deserves to stand in that proud rank. There is the buoyant spirit of youth in every line, in the rapturous intoxication of hope, and in the bitterness of despair. . . . Romeo and Juliet are in love, but they are not love-sick. . . .

Romeo is Hamlet in love. There is the same exuberance of passion and sentiment in the one, that there is of thought and sentiment in the other. Both are absent and self-involved, both live out of themselves in a world of imagination. Hamlet is abstracted from everything; Romeo is abstracted from everything but his love, and lost in it. His "frail thoughts dally with faint surmise," and are fashioned out of the suggestions of hope, "the flatteries of sleep." He is himself only in his Juliet; she is his only reality, his heart's true home and idol. The rest of the world is to him a passing dream.

> William Hazlitt, in F. E. Halliday, ed., *Shakespeare and His Critics.* New York: Schocken Books, 1963.

Twentieth-Century Criticism

Romeo and Juliet as a Dramatic Experiment

The plot of *Romeo and Juliet* is pure fiction. . . . Moreover the hero and the heroine had none of the pomp of historic circumstance about them; they were socially of the minor aristocracy who were to stock

Shakespeare's comedies, and their only political significance was an adventitious role in the civic disturbance of a small city-state. Romeo and Juliet were in effect just a boy and a girl in a novel; and as such they had no claim to the world's attention, except through their passion and their fate.

To choose such folk as these for Tragic heroes was aesthetically well-nigh an anarchist's gesture; and the dramatist provided a sort of programme-prologue to prompt the audience to see the play from the right point of view. In this play-bill the dramatist draws special attention to two features of his story. First, Verona was being torn by a terrible, bloodthirsty feud which no human endeavour had been able to settle; this was the direct cause of the death of the lovers, and but for those deaths it never would have been healed. Second, the course of the young lovers' lives is from the outset governed by a malignant destiny; fatal, star-crossed, death-marked, they are doomed to piteous destruction.

The intent of this emphasis is clear. The tale must end with the death of two ravishingly attractive young folk. . . . [Shakespeare] disowns responsibility for this and throws it on Destiny, Fate. The device is well warranted in the tragic and especially in its Senecan models. But whether in fact it succeeds is a matter for further consideration. The invocation of Fate is strengthened by the second feature scored heavily in the prologue, the feud. The feud is so to speak the means by which Fate acts. The feud is to provide the sense of immediate, and Fate that of ultimate, inevitability.

Is then Shakespeare's *Romeo and Juliet* an unsuccessful experiment? To say so may seem not only to profane but foolish. In its own day, as the dog-eared Bodley Folio [the first collection of Shakespeare's plays] shows, and ever since, it has been one of Shakespeare's most preferred plays. It is indeed rich in spells of its own. But as a pattern of the idea of tragedy, it is a failure. Even Shakespeare appears to have felt that, as an experiment, it had disappointed him.

> H. B. Charlton, in F. E. Halliday, ed., *Shakespeare and His Critics*. New York: Schocken Books, 1963.

The Role of Courtly Love in *Romeo and Juliet*

Romeo and Juliet is a love story, but in Shakespeare's day love included many complex rituals. Early in the Middle ages a cult had developed called Courtly Love, which focused on a curious etiquette that became a kind of parody of Christian experience. Someone might be going about his business, congratulating himself on not being caught in the trap of a love affair, when suddenly the God of Love, Eros or Cupid, angry at being left out of things, forces him to fall in love with a woman. The falling in love is involuntary and instantaneous, no more "romantic," in the usual sense, than getting shot with a bullet. It's never gradual: "Who ever loved that loved not at first sight?" says Marlowe, in a line that Shakespeare quotes in *As You Like It*. From that time on, the lover is the slave of the god of Love, whose will is embodied in his mistress, and he is bound to do whatever she wants.

This cult of love was not originally linked to marriage. Marriage was a relationship in which the man had all the effective authority, even if his wife was (as she usually was) his social equal. The conventional role of the Courtly Love mistress was to be proud, disdainful, and "cruel," repelling all advances from her lover. The frustration this caused drove the lover into poetry, and the theme of the poetry was the cruelty of the mistress and the despair and supplications of the lover. It's good psychology that a creative impulse to write poetry can arise from sexual frustration, and Elizabethan poets almost invariably were or pretended to be submerged in unhappy love, and writing for that reason.

By Shakespeare's time the convention [of Courtly Love] had become more [accepted], was much more frequently linked to eventual marriage, and the more overtly sexual aspects of such relationships were more fully explored. So "love" in *Romeo and Juliet* covers three different forms of a convention. First, the orthodox [Courtly Love] convention in Romeo's professed love for Rosaline at the beginning of the play. Second, the less sublimated love for which the only honourable resolution was marriage, represented by the main theme of the play. Third, the more cynical and ribald perspective that we get in Mercutio's comments, and perhaps those of the Nurse as well.

> Northrop Frye, *Northrop Frye on Shakespeare*. New Haven,
> CT: Yale University Press, 1986.

Fate and Love

The love [Shakespeare] describes [in *Romeo and Juliet*] is of itself beautiful and valuable; but just as it is in the very nature the business of the young, with passions hardly controlled, so is it in its very nature associated with disaster and death. Portents, whether of the stars or of dreams, will foretell it. . . . Caught in the tragic of events . . . Romeo fluctuates from melancholy to high spirits, from unmanly despair to calm, and moves from recognition that it is "e'en so" to a kind of adult fatalism. Juliet more strikingly changes from a girl too young to have thoughts of marriage into a mature and suffering woman.

It is in this sense that we should understand the emphasis on Fate. It is represented in the law of the world, which neither the dateless passion of the lovers nor the expedients of Friar Lawrence can alter. Fortune throws the characters into attitudes which ironically belie their fine words; the Friar says "wisely and slow" but acts in haste, stumbles, leaves Juliet to her unnecessary fate; the lovers who have found the real thing share but one brief night together; Romeo, seeking to end the feud, is forced to kill Tybalt.

Frank Kermode, in *The Riverside Shakespeare*. Boston: Houghton Mifflin, 1974.

Romeo and Juliet: Flawed Excellence

Romeo and Juliet differs in one important respect from the other tragedies. Although it is marked by intense passion and although its tragic course is at least in part due to the most irresistible of all emotions, love, the two protagonists are not of the tragic stature found in the other plays. Romeo, it is true, kills, besides himself, two other men, and Juliet kills herself. But neither is imposingly built on a large scale, and they are, perforce, more passive than active. They are the victims of what the opening chorus calls "piteous overthrows." So we can feel pity, but not terror, at their fates.

This is not to say that the play is inferior to or less moving than the others. It is perfect in its kind. It shows pure, youthful, tragic love in a poetry consummately suited to that love. The pity is poignant enough to evoke tears, as it often does, in an audience. And the characters, though less complex as well as less grand than those that Shakespeare would create in his maturity, are perfect for their roles and perhaps more compellingly lovable than any others. . . . Most important in assessing both the quality and the tragic effect of the play is the fact that it belongs to one of the most dependably heartrending of genres in all world literature: *Liebestod,* or love-death.

Paul A. Jorgensen, *William Shakespeare: The Tragedies*. Boston: Twayne, 1985.

Romeo, Juliet, and the Capulet-Montague Feud

Romeo and Juliet is about a pair of adolescents trying to grow up. Growing up requires that they separate themselves from their parents by forming an intimate bond with one of the opposite sex which supercedes filial bonds. This, broadly, is an essential task of adolescence, in Renaissance England or Italy as in America today. . . . The feud in a realistic social sense is the primary tragic force in the play—not the feud as agent of fate. . . . The feud is the deadly *rite-de-passage* which promotes masculinity at the price of life. Undeniably, the feud is bound up with a pervasive sense of fatedness. . . .

The feud is first referred to in the play as "their parents' strife and their parents' rage" and it is clear that the fathers, not their children, are responsible for its continuance. Instead of providing social channels and moral guidance by which the energies of youth can be rendered beneficial to themselves and society, the Montagues and the Capulets make weak gestures toward civil peace while participating emotionally in the feud as much as their children do. While they fail to exercise authority over the younger generation in the streets, they wield it selfishly and stubbornly at home. So many of the faults of character which critics have found in Romeo and Juliet are shared by their parents that the play cannot be viewed as a tragedy of character in the Aristotelian sense, in which the tragedy results because the hero and heroine fail to "love moderately." Rather, the feud's ambiance of hot temper permeates age as well as youth; viewed from the standpoint of Prince Escalus who embodies the law, it is Montague and Capulet who are childishly refractory.

> Coppelia Kahn, in Mark Rose, ed., *Shakespeare's Early Tragedies.*
> Englewood Cliffs, NJ: Prentice Hall, 1995.

Romeo and Revenge

Romeo's relationship to Tybalt is somewhat similar to Hamlet's relationship to Laertes: both male protagonists are reluctant avengers who must confront more eager avengers as enemy. The tragedy of *Hamlet* is that the male protagonist dies at the moment he is fit to be king. Despite his transcendence of the revenge code, his world is governed by it. Like Hamlet at his duel with Laertes, Romeo at his duel with Paris has surpassed the code of revenge. *Romeo and Juliet* would be a comedy if Romeo were challenged merely to break through the boundaries of his role as chivalric lover because Juliet successfully tutors him in the realm of intimate relations. But the play is a tragedy because he is challenged to break out of his role as chivalric avenger as well, and Juliet's effect upon him is insufficient in this sphere. *Romeo and Juliet* is a tragedy instead of a comedy because Romeo kills Tybalt before he breaks out of the role of avenger.

> Evelyn Gajowski, *The Art of Loving.* Newark:
> University of Delaware Press, 1992.

Comedy and Tragedy

Romeo and Juliet is different from Shakespeare's other tragedies in that it becomes, rather than is, tragic. Other tragedies have reversals, but in *Romeo and Juliet* the reversal is so radical as to constitute a change of genre: the action and the characters begin in familiar comic patterns, and are then transformed—or discarded—to compose the pattern of tragedy.

Comedy and tragedy, being opposed ways of apprehending the real world, project their own opposing worlds. The tragic world is governed by inevitability, and its highest value is personal integrity. In the comic world "evitability" is assumed; instead of heroic or obstinate adherence to a single course, comedy endorses opportunistic shifts and realistic accommodations as means to an end of new social health. The differing laws of comedy and tragedy point to opposed concepts of law itself. Law in the comic world is extrinsic, imposed on society *en masse*. Its source there is usually human, so that law may either be stretched ingeniously to suit the character's ends, or flouted, or even annulled by benevolent rulers. . . . Even deep-rooted social laws, like the obedience owed to parents by their children, are constantly overturned. But in the tragic world law is inherent: imposed by the individual's own nature, it may direct him to a conflict with the larger patterns of law inherent in the universe. . . . Tragic law cannot be altered; it does no good to tell destruction to stop breeding destruction, or to tell gods or human individuals to stop being themselves.

In these opposed worlds our sense of time and its value also differs. . . . The events of tragedy . . . acquire urgency in their uniqueness and their irrevocability; they will never happen again, and one by one they move the hero closer to the end of his own time in death.

> Susan Snyder, in Mark Rose, ed., *Shakespeare's Early Tragedies.*
> Englewood Cliffs, NJ: Prentice Hall, 1995.

The Theatrical Experience of *Romeo and Juliet*

Everything in *Romeo and Juliet* is intense, impatient, threatening, explosive. We are caught up in speed, heat, desire, riots, running, jumping, rapid-fire puns, dirty jokes, extravagance, compressed and urgent passion, the pressure of secrets, fire, blood, death. Visually, the play remains memorable for a number of repeated images—street brawls, swords flashing to hand, torches rushing on and off, crowds rapidly gathering. The upper stage is used frequently, with many opportunities for leaping and scrambling or stretching up and down and much play between upper and lower areas. The dominant bodily feelings we get as an audience are oppressive heat, sexual desire, a frequent whiz-bang exhilarating kinesthesia of speed and clash, and above all a feeling of the keeping down and separation of highly charged bodies, whose pressure toward release and whose sudden discharges determine the rhythm of the play.

> Michael Goldman, in Mark Rose, ed., *Shakespeare's Early Tragedies*. Englewood Cliffs, NJ: Prentice Hall, 1995.

The Influence of Sonnets

From the first spoken words of *Romeo and Juliet*, the Chorus' speech in sonnet-form, we are directed to a major source for the play's language, the sonnet tradition, from which, as we see at once, Romeo had drunk deep. . . . Romeo knew the literary modes of the Renaissance young gentleman. Critics of the play speak again and again of the sonnets in the play itself, sometimes even a full fourteen lines spoken by a speaker alone or by two speakers in consort—the great sonnet exchange between Romeo and Juliet at their meeting is a sign both of their rhetorical sophistication and of their union with one another. Some of the sonnets have an extra quatrain or even sestet; once an octave stands alone, several times a sestet stands alone. All this sonnet-formality must draw our attention to what the playwright was up to—that is, his deepening of events by a language habitually associated with a particular kind of high-minded and devoted love. By his borrowing of devices and language from another genre for his tragedy, he cues us to the kind of love involved in his play. Of all the lyric forms, indeed literary forms, of love, the sonnet-sequence honors the profound seriousness of the emotion: love is central to the life and existence of the sonnet-persona, who gives himself over to the delicious exigencies of his condition, which he celebrates with all the force of his soul and of his poetical powers. As more transitory love-lyrics do not, the sonnet-sequence also provides opportunities for deep and faceted self-examination, as the sonneteer considers and reconsiders his ever-changing emotional state, recording as carefully as possible his perceptions of his own shifting progress and regress along his path.

> Rosalie Colie, in Mark Rose, ed., *Shakespeare's Early Tragedies*. Englewood Cliffs, NJ: Prentice Hall, 1995.

Chronology

1558
The coronation of Queen Elizabeth.

1564
William Shakespeare is born on April 23 to John and Mary Shakespeare in Stratford-upon-Avon.

1570
Queen Elizabeth is excommunicated by Pope Pius V.

1573
Henry Wriothesley, earl of Southhampton, is born; he will later become Shakespeare's patron.

1577
Sir Francis Drake begins his voyage around the world; John Shakespeare's fortunes begin to decline and he sinks into debt; William is withdrawn from school and probably put to work as an apprentice in his father's shop.

1580
Drake returns from his voyage in triumph after attacking Spanish ships and capturing tremendous booty.

1582
William Shakespeare, age eighteen, marries Anne Hathaway, age twenty-six; she is already three months' pregnant.

1583
Susanna, Shakespeare's first child, is born and baptized on May 26.

1584
Sir Walter Raleigh's expedition to inspect North America for colonization is a failure.

1585
English colonists are sent to Roanoke Island, Virginia, and disappear under mysterious circumstances; Hamnet and Judith, Shakespeare's twin son and daughter, are born and baptized on February 2; Shakespeare leaves Stratford for unknown reasons.

1587
Mary, Queen Elizabeth's Catholic half-sister, is executed on the queen's order; Sir Francis Drake attacks and cripples the Spanish fleet at Cadiz.

1588
The Spanish Armada is defeated by the British navy; patriotic fervor is at an all-time high in England.

1589
Shakespeare's first play, *Henry VI Part 1*, is written and performed to popular acclaim.

1591
Tea is first introduced into England.

1592
The bubonic plague strikes London and the public theaters are closed; jealous about Shakespeare's success, Robert Greene attacks him in his *A Groatsworth of Wit* as an "upstart crow."

1593
Shakespeare dedicates "Venus and Adonis" to Henry Wriothesley, earl of Southampton, in an attempt to secure his patronage.

1594
Shakespeare dedicates "The Rape of Lucrece," the sequel to "Venus and Adonis," to the earl of Southampton; he begins writing the *Sonnets*.

1595
The plague eases, and London's public theaters are opened for business; Shakespeare becomes associated with the Lord Chamberlain's Men as a "sharer" (stockholder); he reportedly purchases his share with money given to him by Southampton.

1596
The Shakespeare family is granted a coat of arms; Hamnet, Shakespeare's only son, dies and is buried on August 11.

1597
A second Spanish Armada is scattered by bad weather before it can reach England; Shakespeare purchases a home, "New Place," in Stratford and fails to pay his taxes in London.

1598
Francis Meres praises Shakespeare's skill in *Palladis Tamia*; the Theatre in Shoreditch is torn down and transported to Bankside, where it is reconstructed and renamed the Globe.

1599
The Globe opens in Bankside; it becomes the theater commonly

associated with the Lord Chamberlain's Men and the name of William Shakespeare.

1601

Essex attempts to overthrow Queen Elizabeth but fails and is executed; the earl of Southampton is imprisoned for his role in the revolt; John Shakespeare, William's father, dies; the Lord Chamberlain's Men are investigated for their role in Essex's failed rebellion.

1602

Shakespeare buys land and homes in Stratford; his right to possess a coat of arms is attacked.

1603

Queen Elizabeth dies, and King James of Scotland becomes the new ruler of England; after James assumes the throne, the Lord Chamberlain's Men are issued a royal license and change their name to the King's Men in honor of their new patron; the plague ravages London, and public theaters are closed.

1604

Since Shakespeare is a member of the King's Men and, subsequently, a member of James's household, he is granted four yards of red cloth for a royal procession through London.

1605

Catesby's Gunpowder Plot to blow up the English Parliament as King James addressed it is discovered and foiled; Shakespeare purchases a half-interest in tithes (profits from the farms) in Old Stratford, Welcombe, and Bishopton.

1607

Captain John Smith establishes Jamestown in the colony of Virginia; Susanna, Shakespeare's older daughter, marries Dr. John Hall on June 5; Shakespeare's youngest brother, Edmund, dies in London and is buried on December 31.

1608

Elizabeth Hall, Shakespeare's first granddaughter, is born and baptized on February 21; Shakespeare's mother, Mary, dies and is buried on September 9; Shakespeare sues John Addenbrooke for debt and becomes a one-seventh sharer in the new Blackfriars Theatre; Blackfriars becomes the second, and more profitable, home for the King's Men.

1609
Shakespeare's *Sonnets* is published without authorization.

1610
Shakespeare returns to Stratford and begins semiretirement.

1611
The King James Bible is first published; Shakespeare is in court with other citizens to defend his Stratford tithes; he writes *The Tempest*, his "farewell" play.

1612
Shakespeare is called as a witness in a lawsuit brought against Christopher Mountjoy by his son-in-law Stephen Belott about the terms of an arranged marriage to Mountjoy's daughter; Shakespeare's brother Gilbert dies and is buried on February 3.

1613
Shakespeare's only surviving brother, Richard, dies and is buried on February 4; in London, Shakespeare purchases the Blackfriars Gatehouse; Shakespeare and Richard Burbage (Shakespeare's business partner) are each paid forty-four shillings for making an "impressa" (an emblem or motto).

1614
Shakespeare plays a small role in a lawsuit to oppose the enclosure of lands in Welcombe that would affect his tithes.

1616
Shakespeare's younger daughter, Judith, marries Thomas Quiney; less than a month later, Quiney is summoned to court on fornication charges and a public scandal ensues; Shakespeare becomes ill with an unknown sickness; sensing that death is near, Shakespeare revises his will and dies on April 23.

1623
A monument to Shakespeare is established in the Holy Trinity Church of Stratford; Shakespeare's wife, Anne dies; the First Folio, a collection of nearly all of Shakespeare's plays, is first published in November by his friends Heminge and Condell.

Chronology of Shakespeare's Works

1589–1590	*Henry VI Part 1*
1590–1591	*Henry VI Part 2*
1590–1591	*Henry VI Part 3*
1590–1593	*Titus Andronicus*
1590–1593	*Sir Thomas More*
1592–1593	*Richard III*
1592–1593	*The Comedy of Errors*
1592–1593	"Venus and Adonis"
1593–1594	"The Rape of Lucrece"
1593–1594	*The Taming of the Shrew*
1593–1595	*Sonnets*
1594	*The Two Gentlemen of Verona*
1594–1595	*Love's Labor's Lost*
1594–1595	*King John*
1595	*Richard II*
1595–1596	*Romeo and Juliet*
1595–1596	*A Midsummer Night's Dream*
1596–1597	*The Merchant of Venice*
1596–1597	*Henry IV Part 1*
1597	*The Merry Wives of Windsor*
1598	*Henry IV Part 2*
1598–1599	*Much Ado About Nothing*
1599	*Henry V*
1599	*Julius Caesar*
1599	*As You Like It*
1600–1601	*Hamlet*
1601	"The Phoenix and the Turtle"
1601	*Twelfth Night*
1601–1602	*Troilus and Cressida*
1602–1603	*All's Well That Ends Well*

1604	*Measure for Measure*
1604	*Othello*
1605	*King Lear*
1606	*Macbeth*
1606	*Antony and Cleopatra*
1607–1608	*Coriolanus*
1607–1608	*Timon of Athens*
1607–1608	*Pericles*
1609–1610	*Cymbeline*
1610–1611	*The Winter's Tale*
1611	*The Tempest*
1612	*Henry VIII*
1612–1613	*Cardenio*
1613	*The Two Noble Kinsmen*

Works Consulted

Editions of *Romeo and Juliet*

The Tragedy of Romeo and Juliet has been widely published over the last four hundred years, and many different versions of the play are available. Students of Shakespeare should secure an annotated, unabridged, uncensored version of the play. Paperback versions that meet these criteria are available at most major bookstores.

The Riverside Shakespeare (G. Blakemore Evans, ed., Boston: Houghton Mifflin, 1974) is the version favored by scholars, critics, and biographers. This anthology contains complete versions of Shakespeare's plays and poems, illustrations, records of Shakespeare's life, and introductory essays for each play and poem. *The Riverside Shakespeare* also contains criticism written by Shakespeare's contemporaries. It is the version that was used for compiling this book.

Biographies

Edmund Chambers, *A Short Life of Shakespeare with the Sources.* Ed. Charles Williams. London: Oxford University Press, 1963. An excellent abridged version of Edmund Chamber's two-volume biography of William Shakespeare.

Dennis Kay, *William Shakespeare: His Life and Times.* New York: Twayne, 1995. Respected Renaissance scholar Dennis Kay examines William Shakespeare's life and the world he lived in.

A. L. Rowse, *Shakespeare the Man.* New York: St. Martin's Press, 1988. A. L. Rowse is a celebrated Elizabethan historian who has written extensively on Renaissance England and William Shakespeare. His biography is an excellent source for information on Shakespeare.

S. Schoenbaum, *William Shakespeare: A Compact Documentary Life.* New York: Oxford University Press, 1987. S. Schoenbaum is a professor of Renaissance studies at the University of Maryland and has written a couple of biographies of William Shakespeare.

Thomas Thrasher, *The Importance of William Shakespeare.* San Diego: Lucent Books, 1999. A biography of Shakespeare that includes illustrations and a chronology of his life and plays.

Katherine Baker Siepmann, ed., *Benet's Reader's Encyclopedia.* 3rd ed. New York: Harper and Row, 1987. This book provides the reader with everything from definitions of literary terms to author biographies to summaries of literary works.

Historical Background

William L. Lace, *Elizabethan England*. San Diego: Greenhaven Press, 1995. A history of the events of Elizabethan England.

Jill L. Levenson, *Shakespeare in Performance:* Romeo and Juliet. Wolfeboro, NH: Manchester University Press, 1987. A stage history of *Romeo and Juliet* from the Renaissance to 1968.

The Shakespeare Resource Page (http://daphne.palomar.edu/ SHAKESPEARE) This web site contains the complete works of William Shakespeare, a brief biography of the bard, some literary criticism, and links to other Shakespearean sites.

E. M. W. Tillyard, *The Elizabethan World Picture*. New York: Vintage Books, ca. 1942. A brief account of the ideas that shaped the Elizabethan mind. It covers such topics as the Chain of Being, the Four Elements, the Four Humours, and the Cosmic Dance.

Diane Yancey, *Life in the Elizabethan Theater*. San Diego: Greenhaven Press, 1997. This book explores what life would be like for a person who worked in the theater during Shakespeare's time.

Literary Criticism

M. H. Abrams, ed., *The Norton Anthology of English Literature*. Vol. 1. 6th ed. New York: W. W. Norton, 1993. This exhaustive two-volume set is a basic university-level text covering a major portion of English literature. It contains selective critical essays on William Shakespeare and a good sampling of his works. *The Norton Anthology* contains annotations and a glossary.

Victor L. Cahn, *Shakespeare the Playwright*. New York: Greenwood Press, 1991. An easy-to-read book that offers guidance in understanding each of Shakespeare's plays.

Joseph S. M. J. Chang, "The Language of Paradox in *Romeo and Juliet,*" *Shakespeare Studies*. 1967. This essay examines the use of paradoxes in *Romeo and Juliet*.

Gareth Lloyd Evans, *The Upstart Crow: An Introduction to Shakespeare's Plays*. London: J. M. Dent and Sons, 1982. This book offers essays that explore each of Shakespeare's plays and offers direction for understanding them.

Levi Fox, *The Shakespeare Handbook*. Boston: G. K. Hall, 1987. An excellent book that provides summaries of William Shakespeare's works.

Northrop Frye, *Northrop Frye on Shakespeare*. Ed. Robert Sandler. New Haven, CT: Yale University Press, 1986. An interesting and easy-to-read book in which the renowned literary critic Northrop Frye offers his views on several of Shakespeare's most famous plays.

Evelyn Gajowski, *The Art of Loving: Female Subjectivity and Male Discursive Traditions in Shakespeare's Tragedies.* Newark: University of Delaware Press, 1992. This book examines the role that women play in Shakespeare's tragedies.

F. E. Halliday, ed., *Shakespeare and His Critics.* New York: Schocken Books, 1963. This anthology contains more than three hundred years of critical commentary on Shakespeare and his plays and poems.

Alfred Harbage, ed., *Shakespeare: The Tragedies.* Englewood Cliffs, NJ: Prentice Hall, 1964. This anthology offers critical comments on Shakespeare's tragedies by respected early-twentieth-century critics.

Paul A. Jorgensen, *William Shakespeare: The Tragedies.* Boston: Twayne, 1985. Written by a respected Shakespeare scholar, this book scrutinizes several of Shakespeare's key plays in terms of theme, plot, character, and symbol.

Jill L. Levenson, "The Definition of Love: Shakespeare's Phrasing in *Romeo and Juliet,*" *Shakespeare Studies.* 1982. This essay surveys the influence that the courtly love tradition had on *Romeo and Juliet.*

H. A. Mason, *Shakespeare's Tragedies of Love.* London: Chatto and Windus, 1970. This book probes four of Shakespeare's tragedies that revolve around the theme of love.

Joseph A. Porter, ed., *Critical Essays on Shakespeare's* Romeo and Juliet. New York: G. K. Hall, 1997. This book contains a collection of essays that consider various aspects of *Romeo and Juliet.*

Mark Rose, ed., *Shakespeare's Early Tragedies: A Collection of Critical Essays.* Englewood Cliffs, NJ: Prentice Hall, 1995. This collection of essays covers Shakespeare's first tragedies and offers critical insights on them.

Marilyn L. Williamson, "Romeo and Death," *Shakespeare Studies.* 1981. This essay questions Romeo's motives for committing suicide.

Index

Picture Credits

About the Author

Thomas Thrasher lives in Long Beach with his cat, Jinx, and a 1965 Falcon. He teaches at Rio Hondo College in Whittier and at California State University, Long Beach. He also likes to dabble in poetry and fiction.